SKILLS IN RELIGIOUS STUDIES

book 3

S C MERCIER

HEINEMANN
EDUCATIONAL

Heinemann Educational Publishers
Halley Court, Jordan Hill, Oxford OX2 8EJ
a division of Reed Educational & Professional Publishing Ltd

MELBOURNE AUCKLAND FLORENCE PRAGUE
MADRID ATHENS SINGAPORE TOKYO
SÃO PAULO CHICAGO PORTSMOUTH (NH)
MEXICO IBADAN GABORONE JOHANNESBURG
KAMPALA NAIROBI

© S. C. Mercier 1990

First published 1990

97 98 11 10 9 8
British Library Cataloguing in Publication Data

Mercier, S. C.
    Skills in religious studies.
    Bk. 3
    1. Religion
    I. Title
    291

ISBN 0 435 30202 7

Typeset and illustrated by Gecko Limited, Bicester, Oxon

Printed and bound in Spain by Mateu Cromo

Acknowledgements

Thanks are due to the following for commenting on the manuscript: M.M. Ahsan, Douglas Charing, W. Owen Cole, Arye Forta, Anil D. Goonewardene, Janey Graham, V.P. (Hemant) Kanitkar, V. Khadke, Peggy Morgan, S.H. Rehman and Piara Singh Sambhi.

The author would also like to thank Jo Fageant for her consultation on the photographs, and V.P. (Hemant) Kanitkar for his translation of the prayer on p. 12.

The publishers would like to thank the following for permission to reproduce photographs: J.C. Allen pp. 53 (B), 56 (A); Andes Press Agency/Carlos Reyes pp. 7 (C), 54 (A), 55 (B), 57 (B); Barnaby's Picture Library pp. 15 (B), 19 (C), 29 (C), 30 (D), 35 (B), 45 (C), 79 (C), 80 (A); Barnaby's Picture Library/Juliette Soester p. 30 (A); Robin Bath p. 41 (B); Robin Bath/Andy Webber p. 39 (B); British Museum p. 40 (A); Keith Ellis p.90; Format Photographers/Jacky Chapman p. 6 (A); Format Photographers/Maggie Murray p. 63 (B); Format Photographers/Val Wilmer p. 58 (A, B); Sally and Richard Greenhill pp. 6 (B), 16 (B), 18 (A), 19 (B), 36 (A), 52 (A), 62 (A), 68 (A), 71 (B), 78 (B), 80–81 (B); Sonia Halliday Photographs p. 91; Sonia Halliday Photographs/Barry Searle p. 28 (A); Robert Harding Picture Library pp. 8 (A), 8–9 (B), 28 (B), 38 (A), 42 (A), 42–43 (B), 65–66 (C), 72 (A), 78 (A); Hutchison Library pp. 10 (A), 10–11 (B), 12 (A), 13 (B), 22 (A), 31 (C), 44 (A, B), 46 (A, B), 46–47 (C), 59 (C), 60 (A), 61 (B), 69 (B), 70 (A), 84 (A), 84–85 (B), 86 (A); Christine Osborne Pictures p. 74 (A); Christine Osborne Pictures/MEP pp. 88 (A), 89 (B); Ann and Bury Peerless pp. 21 (B, C), 82 (A), 83 (B), 87 (B); Petit Format/Nestle/Science Photo Library p. 4 (A); David Richardson p. 15 (A); Peter Sanders pp. 64 (A), 65 (B), 66 (A), 67 (Bi, Bii), 73 (B), 75 (B), 77 (C); Peter Sanders/John Gulliver pp. 76 (A), 77 (B); Zefa Picture Library (UK) Ltd pp. 4 (B), 16 (A), 17 (C), 21 (C), 23 (B), 24 (A), 25 (B), 26 (A), 26–27 (B), 32 (A), 33 (B), 34–35 (A), 36–37 (B), 48 (A), 51 (B).

Cover photographs by: Andes Press Agency/Carlos Reyes (front, centre); Sally and Richard Greenhill (front, left); Robert Harding Picture Library Ltd (back, centre and front, right); Hutchison Library (back, left); Zefa Picture Library (UK) Ltd (back, right).

Contents

1 Life maps 4
2 Stages in life 6

Hinduism

3 Hinduism: one soul, many lives 8
4 Before birth 10
5 Hindu birth ceremonies 12
6 The Sacred Thread ceremony 14
7 Love and marriage 16
8 A Hindu wedding 18
9 Hindu cremation 20

Judaism

10 Judaism: celebrating life 22
11 The path to holiness 24
12 Brit Milah 26
13 Bar Mitzvah 28
14 Bat Mitzvah 30
15 Marriage in the Jewish tradition 32
16 A Jewish funeral 34

Buddhism

17 Buddhism: life as an endless cycle 36
18 Two paths, one way 38
19 Buddhism and popular custom 40
20 Growing up in Buddhist society 42
21 Initiation 44
22 Buddhism and marriage 46
23 Death rites in Buddhism 48

Christianity

24 Christianity: the journey of life 50
25 Infant Baptism 52
26 Growing in the faith 54
27 Confirmation 56
28 Believer's Baptism 58
29 Christian marriage 60
30 Death 62

Islam

31 Islam: freedom to choose 64
32 Birth and naming 66
33 Growing up in Islam 68
34 Preparing for marriage 70
35 A Muslim wedding 72
36 Life after death 74
37 Muslim funeral rites 76

Sikhism

38 Sikhism: many lives, one journey 78
39 The Sikh naming ceremony 80
40 Life as a spiritual journey 82
41 Amrit-pan karna 84
42 Sikh marriage 86
43 Death and cremation 88

44 Further study 90
Glossary 92
Bibliography and resources 96

1

Life maps

There are many things which are uncertain in life. There are, however, two certain points on every life span: the beginning and the end. If we were to draw a chart of a life span, these two points could be marked in. We can also ask questions about these certainties of life, such as:

- Is death the end of life or is it only the end of this particular existence?
- Is our birth our beginning or only the start of this present life?
- Have we had previous lives?
- Will we live again after death?

People have very different ideas about the answers to these questions. They hold different beliefs about the pattern and purpose of life too. Some people believe that life follows a plan and purpose. Others say that it is up to us to find pattern and meaning in our lives.

way things are going. Of course, some people have far more freedom to make significant changes in their lives than others.

We can look at life in different ways. Perhaps we only really get a proper view of life when we have lived a long time. Then we can see things in perspective. When we are very young life seems to stretch out into the distant future. Nevertheless, there are turning points and milestones on the way which we can see ahead of us. These are often times for decisions or for reflection. For example, there are turning points in school life when you have to make decisions about what you want to do. This means thinking about your abilities, your character, your outlook and aims in life.

The world's religious traditions interpret life in different ways. In one religion life is seen as part of a never-ending cycle, in another, life is a journey with a definite goal. Looking at the way other people map out human life can help each of us to think about our own life and the way it is going. We may come to very different conclusions from those around us but it is still important to try to understand how others see the pattern of life, its purpose and its meaning.

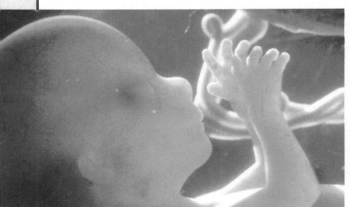

A   A human embryo: does life really begin at birth?

In certain ways the pattern of our lives is already mapped out for us from the beginning. There are things which shape our lives, such as when we are born, our sex, our physical appearance, our environment, our family, our culture, our background or even the religious tradition in which we grow up.

There are some things in life which we cannot change but we are able to shape our lives to some extent. We can strive to fulfil certain hopes and ideals. We can learn a little or a lot. We can be content to let life wash over us or we can try to make important changes in the

B   Elderly people may have a different view of life.

Life maps

1 Draw a diagram of a human life. It can be represented as a journey or a map, as a circle or spiral, a boardgame or a chart. Indicate some of the key points in human life using pictures, symbols or words. Use the example (C) to help you. Share your ideas with a partner and explain your diagram.

2 Look at Photo A. When does life really begin? Is it at birth or before? Discuss this in class. Find out more about the stages in the development of the human foetus. Perhaps you could invite a doctor to come and talk to you about medical views on this difficult question.

3 Make a list of milestones or main turning points in a person's life up to the age of 21, e.g. birth, starting school. Say which turning points are 'given' and which are in the person's control. Discuss these in class.

4 Do you think that you will see life differently when you are much older, as a grandmother or grandfather perhaps? Write a poem or story in which an elderly person looks back on their youth and sees things differently from when they were young.

5 'Life is like an onion; you peel it off layer by layer and sometimes you cry a little.' Write your own sayings about life using everyday things to illustrate your meaning. Plan a class assembly on this theme.

6 Some people are in a better position to make changes in their lives than others. What prevents people from making big changes in their lives? How far can we shape our own lives? Discuss these questions in small groups, then write down your own thoughts and answers and share them in class.

C   A life map.

2

Stages in life

Few of us can remember clearly the time when we were very little. Those who cared for us will have watched with excitement all the important steps in our progress. Many people say it is during these earliest stages that our characters are formed.

A   Starting school.

Adults sometimes say 'School days are the best days of your life'. Yet many of us spend much of our childhood looking forward to being grown up. It seems that adults have more freedom, more choice and more power. In some ways this is true. However, many adults look back on their childhood as a time when they were free from the demands and worries of the adult world.

You might think there ought to be some major turning point at which a child enters adulthood. In fact there are many turning points and stages in this process. Some take the form of physical changes, and these may bring emotional changes too. Some are social

B   New rights and responsibilities at 18.

changes, such as the gaining of new rights and responsibilities under the law (B), or new demands made on us at home and school or by fashion and society at large. Some of the turning points may come about through our own choices and through our own changes in attitudes or beliefs.

If asked to map out how they see their lives ahead of them, many young people look forward to a stage of married life when home, family and work become important. In fact most people do not stop to think seriously about life beyond this time. However, there is life beyond this stage! Many people enjoy 20 or more years of retirement and some say that life begins at retirement, when a person is free from the ties of work and family.

When we look at the beliefs of the world religions we can see that they map out life in different ways. Some of the turning points and milestones may be the same but the signposts are often quite different. All the world's religions recognize that certain times in the life cycle are important. There are special ceremonies and rituals to mark these occasions. In this way the community is reminded of the beliefs and values which guide and give meaning to the lives of its members.

Stages in life

C *A way to find meaning in life.*

THINGS TO DO

1 Find out the ages when the following rights and responsibilities are granted according to the law in this country. The age at which:
- you can be convicted of a criminal offence
- you can buy a pet without a parent present
- you can drink alcohol in a pub
- you can be held fully responsible for a crime
- you can leave home with one parent's consent
- you can drive a moped or motor-cycle
- you can drive a car
- you can choose your own religion
- you can be sent to prison
- you can marry without your parents' consent.

Discuss your findings in class. Which of these age limits would you change? Explain why and share your ideas in class.

2 Do adults look back on their childhood with fondness? What are the good things about being a child? What are the difficulties and disappointments? With a partner draw up a list of each of these and discuss your ideas in class.

3 Young people look forward to a time when they will be regarded as adults. Why is this? Write a short play or poem in which a young person expresses these longings to be an adult.

4 Look at Photo B. What turning point in life is significant here? At what time in a person's life does this occur? List the reasons why this is an important time in a person's life. Discuss your answers in class.

5 For many, the belief that life has a purpose is very important (C). What is the purpose of life? List the different answers to this question and discuss them in class, e.g. to learn to live a good life; to keep the human race going.

6 Many people find their religious faith gives this life meaning and shape. Others find that life can have purpose without any religious belief. Do you think that a religious outlook on life is very different from a non-religious approach? In what ways? Discuss these questions in class.

3

Hinduism: one soul, many lives

Hindus believe that this life is only one of many. They believe that everyone has a soul. The soul lives on after death and takes on a new life in a new body on earth. This means that this life is only a small part of a much longer journey.

According to the Hindu scriptures the journey of a human life can be mapped out into important stages. These stages are called **ashramas** and are explained in the scriptures called the **Laws of Manu**. These teachings were intended for particular groups in Hindu society: the priests or **Brahmins**, the warrior classes or **Kshatriyas** and the merchant or **Vaishya** class.

The four stages in life according to this tradition are:

1 the student stage (**brahma charya**)
2 the householder (**grihastha**)
3 the recluse (**vanaprastha**)
4 the spiritual seeker (**sannyasin**)

The first stage or ashrama begins when the child or young person is old enough to take their religious and spiritual education seriously. The second ashrama starts with marriage and the setting up of a home. The third stage begins when the person's children have married and have children of their own and there is time to devote to religious and spiritual matters. The last stage is only entered into voluntarily. It is the stage of the sannyasin, who renounces the world to live the life of a recluse or forest-dweller. The sannyasin follows a life of self discipline, asceticism and meditation in order to seek **moksha** or liberation from the cycle of reincarnation (A).

A   The way of the sannyasin

Hinduism: one soul, many lives

Hindu grandparents with their family.

1 Draw a chart or map of life showing the Hindu ashramas. Write an explanation of your drawing. Use the new vocabulary.

2 With a partner, list ways in which the Hindu map of life differs from how you see the stages of life. Discuss the similarities. Share your findings in class.

3 Put the four ashramas as headings at the top of four columns. Under each column write down some of the activities, duties and responsibilities you think might fall under each stage. Discuss your ideas in class.

Duties for stages in life			
Brahma charya	Grihastha	Vanaprastha	Sannyasin
To listen with respect to the words of the teacher or guru			

With each stage there are important responsibilities to be fulfilled. These are a person's duty or **dharma**. Dharma means 'What is right'. In the scriptures it says that it is more important to fulfil one's own dharma, no matter how humble, than to try to carry out the dharma of someone else. Hindus do not all follow the teachings of the Laws of Manu yet the lives of many Hindus today are still influenced by the main ideas behind these teachings. They were written at a time when Hindu society was organized according to class and caste and the stages in life were considered important for the smooth running and well-being of the whole community.

4 Find out more about the Hindu teaching on dharma. You may want to use some of the books suggested in the bibliography on page 96.

5 Work with a partner on an interview. One of you is the Hindu grandmother or grandfather in Photo B. The other is conducting an interview for local radio. Ask the grandparent questions about how the teaching of the scriptures has influenced the way they have lived their life and the way they see life now.

6 Look at Photo A. What sort of life does the sannyasin lead? Revise or look again at the life of the sannyasin. Use the books in the bibliography on page 96 to write a paragraph on the subject.

4

Before birth

Many religious traditions have a special ceremony to mark the birth of a child. In Hinduism there are special rituals even before the child is born. These are centred upon the mother-to-be. At about the fifth or seventh month of pregnancy in some Hindu families the female relatives perform a special ceremony in which the expectant mother is garlanded with flowers and then anointed with perfume and scented oils. She is presented with dishes of the tastiest foods in order to satisfy all her cravings and is encouraged to try every one. The women sing traditional songs and join together in a festive meal. They wish the mother a safe pregnancy and express hopes for a healthy baby. Prayers are said to ask the gods to protect the mother and child.

B   Worship begins in the home.

A   Fire is an important symbol.

During the pregnancy the expectant parents offer gifts and prayers at the shrine in the home or at the local temple. In some Hindu households a special ceremony is held around the sacred fire, and ghee, sandalwood, rice, kukum and turmeric are offered into the flames. This ritual fire is called **Havan**. Prayers are said to **Agni**, the god of fire, and to Lord Vishnu the Preserver of life, for the protection of the child.

The parents hope and pray that the child's **karma** will be good and that the baby will be strong and healthy in this life. Hindus believe

Before birth

1 Do you believe that people 'reap what they sow'? What do you think people mean by this expression? Discuss these questions in class.

2 Imagine you are a Hindu mother- or father-to-be. Write a prayer or poem that you might say expressing your hopes and fears for the child you are waiting for.

3 When any child is born it inherits certain things, e.g. characteristics from its parents. List these and discuss them with a partner. Hindus believe the child also inherits karma from previous lives. How would this change your list? What things might this theory of karma help to explain? How would Hindus explain some of the hardships in life? Discuss these questions in class.

4 Look at Photo A. The symbol of fire is used in rituals on many important occasions. With a partner work on the following questions:
  - What are the qualities of fire?
  - For what is it used?
  - How does it both give and take away?
  - What does fire represent?
  - Why do you think it is used in Hindu ceremonies?
  - Why on this occasion?
  - On what occasions that you know is a fire important?

Discuss your answers in class and write a poem or prayer to 'the god of fire'.

5 Imagine you are a Hindu living in India. Your daughter lives in Britain. She and her husband are expecting their first child. Write a letter of congratulation and express all your hopes, prayers and advice to the parents. Then write the daughter's reply, explaining the ceremonies performed during pregnancy.

6 Write down ten words or phrases which you associate with a new-born baby. Share these in class. Use these ideas to write on the subject of 'Birth' or 'A new-born child'.

that the soul is eternal and lives through many lives on earth. Birth is rebirth. It is the beginning of a new life but not a new soul. The soul carries with it the karma or results of actions from previous existences. An unselfish and generous life builds good karma and the benefits are reaped in lives ahead. Selfishness and unkindness in previous existences lead to bad karma being carried over into the next life. For example, a man may have been hurtful towards those less able than himself in a past life. In the next life he may find he is not as able as others. In this way people reap what they sow.

5
Hindu birth ceremonies

The birth rituals and ceremonies of Hinduism were orginally closely linked with the important task of washing the baby after it was born. This cleansing is now carried out by a midwife at home or at the hospital. In the past the priest would have performed the ritual washing of the baby and he would have made offerings to the gods.

Today, once the baby has been washed and the mother is ready to receive visitors, close family members gather to see mother and baby and to offer their congratulations. The priest may be invited to the home to bless the occasion and to recite prayers for the well being of the mother and child. Sometimes the father holds the baby for the first time on this occasion (A) and dips a small gold ornament or ring into some honey and ghee and touches the baby's lips with the sweet mixture. Then he may recite the prayer:

> Oh dear child, I give you this honey and ghee which has been provided by God who is the producer of all the wealth of the world. May you be preserved and protected by God and live in this world for a hundred autumns.

(Translation by V.P. (Hemant) Kanitkar.)

The mother and child are blessed and sprinkled with drops of water by the priest as he recites prayers for their strength and safekeeping. According to Hindu tradition, mother and child should have no physical contact with the outside world for ten days.

The naming ceremony takes place on the twelfth day after the birth. The baby is washed, dressed in new clothes and, traditionally, laid in a swinging cot surrounded by bright ghee lamps. The priest pronounces the name chosen by the family. The name is then proclaimed to everybody present and sweetmeats are shared out. Prayers are said and everyone sings hymns of praise before joining in a festive meal and celebration. In some families a gold or silver ornament is bought for the child, and sometimes the baby's ears are pierced and gold earrings given.

A 'May you be preserved and protected by God . . .'

Hindu birth ceremonies

Not long after the naming ceremony there is another simple ritual when the child is carried outside into the sunshine for the first time. This is usually performed by the father who holds the baby and recites the **Gayatri Mantra** which is the daily prayer of every Hindu:

Let us meditate on the Universal Divine Light. May it illuminate our thoughts and prayers.

Hindu families may observe other ceremonies during the early stages of childhood. The child's first haircut is considered a significant occasion (B) and the first time the baby is able to take solid foods is also celebrated. These landmarks in a baby's development were particularly important in times when many babies did not survive.

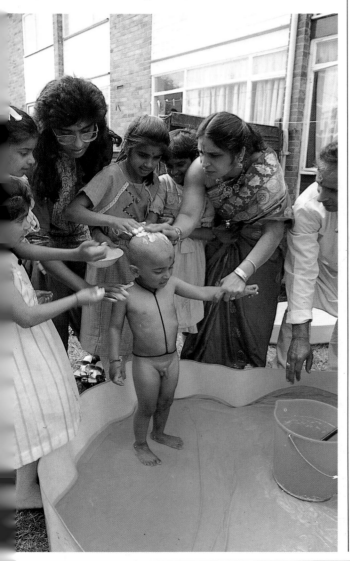

THINGS TO DO

1 Imagine you are a young Hindu. You have a new baby brother. Write a letter to relatives in India who are unable to come over for the birth and describe the special occasions you have celebrated before and after the birth. Try to express some of your excitement and thoughts about the new arrival.

2 List the special occasions in the development of a child from the point of view of most parents. Go through from birth to the first day at school. Think of some ways these occasions might be marked or celebrated.

3 The Gayatri Mantra is said by Hindus each day in their prayers. Think about the hopes it expresses and the intentions of the person who recites it. If you were to recite a poem, saying or prayer each day what hopes and intentions would you want to express? Write yourself such a prayer or saying.

4 Draw or design a card congratulating a Hindu couple on the birth of a child. Use some of the symbols from the ceremonies to help you in your design. Write some appropriate words or message inside.

5 Act out a short play in which a Hindu family comes together to celebrate the birth of a baby. Try to communicate some of the feelings, hopes and fears expressed at this important time.

6 Many Hindu ceremonies are for a male child. In the past in most societies it was considered important that there was a son in the family to continue the family name and inheritance. Do you think that there is still a trace of this tradition nowadays? Discuss this in class.

B *There are many landmarks and special occasions in the process of growing up.*

6

The Sacred Thread ceremony

Once a Hindu boy is old enough to take his spiritual education seriously he can embark on the student stage of life. This stage is called **brahma charya**. Entering the student stage is marked by a special ritual when the Hindu boy receives the Sacred Thread worn by Hindu men.

The Sacred Thread ceremony is called **Upanayam**. In the past the young Hindu would leave home at this stage, to become attached to a **guru** or spiritual teacher. The ceremony would have marked a great change in the boy's life. Today, few boys leave home in this way as they receive their general education at school. However, they do not receive their spiritual education in school, so some Hindu families hold the traditional ceremony when the boy is old enough to learn the **Vedas** and to take his religion seriously. He receives lessons from a guru who may be the local priest. Family and close friends are invited to the ceremony which usually take place in the boy's home.

In preparation, the boy's hair is cut, he bathes and puts on clean clothes. He can have no cooked food on the day until after the ceremony. A fire is lit in a container. This represents the presence of God and is the focus of offerings and prayers. Sandalwood, ghee and incense are sprinkled on to the flames. The boy and his father sit at the fire while the priest recites sacred **mantras**. The boy takes certain vows; he promises to be a good student, to obey his teacher, to be self-disciplined and to remain celibate until his student stage is complete. The guru promises to be as a father to the boy. He gives him the Sacred Thread to hold and, word by word, helps him recite a special prayer. He reminds the boy of the sacred nature of the Thread he is receiving and then puts it over the boy's head and one shoulder so that it hangs diagonally across his chest to his right hip. There is one knot in the Thread and three or five strands. The priest teaches the boy the **Gayatri Mantra** from the Vedas. Then the father gives him a secret name and again recites the Gayatri Mantra.

A   Receiving the Sacred Thread.

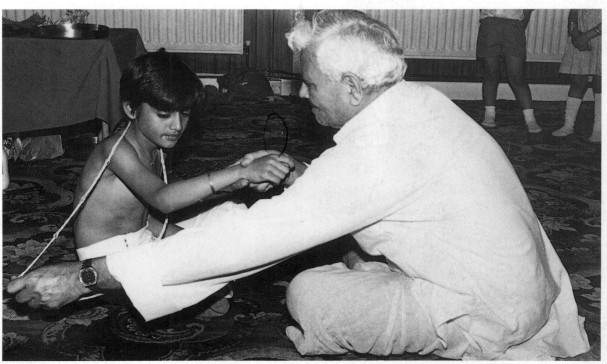

The Sacred Thread ceremony

The Sacred Thread ceremony marks the beginning of the brahma charya stage when the boy takes on full responsibility for his religious life. The priest gives him some words of encouragement and advice for the time of study ahead of him. It will mean self discipline, hard work and perseverence. After the ceremony there is a family celebration and friends and relatives bring gifts for their hosts and for the boy.

B *Prepared for the Sacred Thread ceremony.*

THINGS TO DO

1 Look at the photos. What is happening? How can you tell that this is a serious occasion in the life of the young Hindu? List the points with a partner and share your ideas in class.

2 In what ways does the Sacred Thread ceremony mark a turning point in the boy's life? Do you think this might be the beginning of a difficult time for the boy? In what ways could it be a helpful ceremony for the young person entering a serious stage in life? Discuss this in class.

3 Imagine you are a boy who has just had his Sacred Thread ceremony, or his sister. Write a letter to a friend describing what happened at the Sacred Thread ceremony and say what the occasion means for you and other members of the family.

4 Think about the student stage in the Hindu boy's life. It involves study, respect for teachers, self discipline and thinking about the meaning of life. In what ways does this differ from the stage in life you have reached? In what ways is it similar? Discuss this in class.

5 Revise what you have learned about the Hindu scriptures or look up what you can in the books suggested in the bibliography on page 96. Make up a set of questions about them and exchange papers with a partner. Answer each other's questions.

6 As they grow up young people have many demands made on them by parents, teachers and peers. In what ways can adults support young people as they approach adult life? Write a letter as if to a local paper explaining your feelings on this.

7

Love and marriage

The second stage in life, according to Hindu tradition, begins with marriage. Hindus believe that marriage is a sacrament or sacred ritual. It is seen as an important step in life through which a man and woman can fulfil the holy law of **dharma**. In Hinduism marriage is considered a holy union in which a man and woman share in the creative activity of God through the growing together of two minds and two souls and through the bringing of children into the world.

The story of **Rama** and **Sita** is believed to offer important teaching on Hindu marriage. When Prince Rama gave up the throne to go into exile for 14 years, his faithful wife, Princess Sita, went with him. She gave up the comfort and security of the palace to remain with her husband. During their time in exile Sita was kidnapped by the tyrant King Ravana. He took her to the island of Lanka and tried to persuade her to give up her love for Rama but Sita remained faithful to her husband. Eventually Rama destroyed Ravana and rescued Sita. He took her as his queen back to his rightful kingdom. Both Rama and Sita are seen as models of obedience to dharma and their faithfulness and perseverence in times of separation and difficulty are seen as an example for couples to follow.

In the past Hindu marriage was often arranged between two families. Sometimes marriage was a social necessity. **Arranged marriages** can be found in the history of many societies. Sometimes they were a success and sometimes the marriage was very unhappy but this is true of so-called 'love marriages' too.

Today many Hindu parents would feel they had failed in their duty as parents if they did not make any effort to introduce their children to suitable marriage partners. In fact many Hindu young people are happy to have their parents involved in this way. The son or daughter is consulted at every stage from the introduction to the final decision. If the young person is not happy with the parents' choice then they wait until a more suitable partner is found.

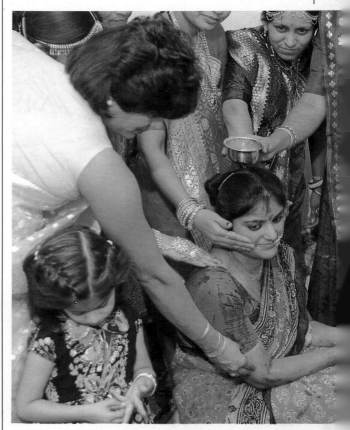

B   Both practical and spiritual preparations are important for the Hindu bride . . .

A   Rama and Sita, who are seen as models for Hindu couples.

Some Hindus choose their own partner, but they usually want their parents to be happy with the decision. Hindu parents prefer their sons and daughters to concentrate on their studies while they are still at school and not to get involved in a relationship. They believe that the dharma of the student must be fulfilled before the next stage in life is begun. This means that 'dating' is often discouraged. When a Hindu marries he or she is marrying into an extended family rather than entering a single relationship. It is important, therefore, that everyone feels happy with the union and can give their support. Once the couple have decided to marry the family priest is consulted to arrange a suitable date for the wedding. The girl's family then attends to all the preparations.

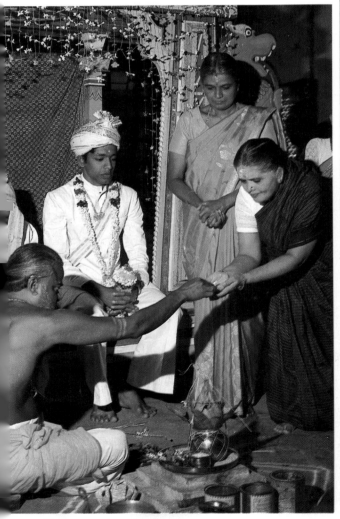

C ... and groom.

Love and marriage

THINGS TO DO

1 What are the different ways in which people find a marriage partner? Are some of these ways more sensible than others? In which of these are parents involved to a greater or lesser degree? Discuss this in class.

2 What are the hopes and fears all parents have when they think about their son or daughter getting engaged or married? Write down as many as you can. Go through your list with a partner and discuss which of these fears are reasonable and which are unreasonable.

3 What things do you think Hindu parents will take into account when looking for a suitable marriage partner for their son or daughter? With a partner discuss whether you agree with these concerns and whether your own parent or guardian would have the same concerns about your choice of marriage partner.

4 Imagine you are a Hindu parent. Write a letter to a close friend or distant relative who has a son a few years older than your daughter, expressing your concerns about finding a marriage partner for your daughter who is just finishing her studies at college.

5 Look again at the story of Rama and Sita and revise what you have learned before. What lessons can the Hindu find in this story about:
   ● dharma
   ● marriage
   ● loyalty
   ● good and evil?
   Write your answers in paragraphs under the heading 'The teachings in the story of Rama and Sita'.

6 Every wedding needs preparation. Look at Photos B and C. What preparations have taken place for this Hindu wedding? What signs are there that this is an important occasion? Answer these questions and discuss them in class.

A Hindu wedding

Before the wedding the Hindu bride is dressed and waited upon by her mother, sisters and other female members of the family. This is a special time for her as she will be leaving her home to move in with her husband's family after the wedding.

In India the marriage is often held in the home of the girl's family. In the UK the Hindu temple or hall in the bride's home town is usually booked for the occasion. The wedding begins with a simple ceremony in which the bride is asked if she has agreed to marry the groom. Once she has affirmed her consent her father places her hand into that of the groom. She receives jewellery and clothes which will remain hers during the marriage. The couple may also receive a gift of money from the girl's family to help in setting up a home.

This simple ritual is followed by a religious ceremony performed by the priest. He prepares the sacred fire for the occasion. As the couple enter, friends and family sing hymns, welcome them with garlands of flowers and shower them with rice grains. A silk curtain is held up between the bride and groom until the ceremony begins. Nowadays they will know each other but in the past they may not have seen each other beforehand.

The bride and groom exchange garlands and sit before the priest at the fire. Offerings of incense and rice are sprinkled on to the flames as the priest calls on the gods, asking their blessing.

The highlight of the ceremony is when the couple take seven steps near the sacred fire. The bride and groom are joined by a silk scarf knotted into their clothing and move round the fire together. With each step a prayer is said. The first may be a prayer for fertility, the second for strength, the third for wealth and prosperity, the fourth for happiness, the fifth for children, the sixth for enjoyment of

A   *The priest asks the blessing of the gods for the bride and groom.*

A Hindu wedding

Marriage marks the couple's entry into the householder stage in life. They must concentrate on setting up a home and earning a living so that they can begin a family and also contribute to the life of the community. In this way they will be fulfilling their **dharma** and benefiting society at large.

B   *Seven steps round the sacred fire, with a prayer for each step.*

pleasures and the seventh for close union. The couple pray that they will live to see a hundred autumns together and live in friendship and harmony. At the end of the ceremony the couple may give each other a sweet cake or spoonful of yoghurt and honey. The wedding is followed by a festive meal with friends and family.

C   *Customs may vary but the same symbols are always used.*

THINGS TO DO

1   What hopes and intentions are expressed in this ceremony? If you were allowed to choose seven prayers or hopes or intentions at your wedding ceremony, what would they be?

2   When they marry, Hindu women receive a small red dot painted on the forehead in make up. There are many other symbols in the Hindu wedding ceremony. Look again at the photos and the text. Draw each of the symbols and write a sentence or two to explain the meaning of each.

3   Imagine you are a sister or brother of the bride at the ceremony. Your teacher has asked you to give a talk about a Hindu wedding. Write up a short talk which describes and explains the ceremony you have watched.

4   In the UK a Hindu couple have to go through a civil wedding at the **register office** before they are considered legally married. Find out what happens at a civil wedding and report back in class. Discuss reasons why a Hindu couple will want a religious wedding after the register office marriage.

5   Find out more about the arrangements, symbols, prayers and rituals of the Hindu marriage ceremony. Use the books in the bibliography on page 96 to help you. Write a mini project on the subject.

6   Design an invitation to a Hindu wedding. Decorate your invitation with suitable Hindu symbols.

9

Hindu cremation

Hindus believe there is one supreme and eternal spirit of the universe; they call this **Brahman**. Hindus also believe that we each have a soul. The soul is called **Atman**. The ultimate aim of every Hindu is to attain **moksha** when the Atman is released from the cycle of rebirth through union with Brahman. Hindu tradition suggests that the last stage in life should be devoted to preparing for death. Once earthly responsibilities have been fulfilled a person can concentrate on spiritual matters: prayer, meditation and reading the scriptures.

Hindus cremate their dead. The symbolism of cremation is important. The body returns to the elements in the form of ashes and the cremation fire ensures the release of the spirit. The spirit will return to earth in another body to live again unless it attains moksha. Sometimes the funeral pyre is built in the open air (A). In the UK a crematorium is used and the ceremony adapted to suit the new circumstances.

When a Hindu dies the body is washed, anointed with sandalwood paste and dressed in clean clothes. One of the sons of the family, often the eldest, is responsible for the arrangements of the cremation. In India he prepares the funeral pyre with firewood. Offerings, too, are prepared including sandalwood, sweet smelling incense and ghee.

A   After this cremation, the ashes will be scattered in the river.

Hindu cremation

The body is carried to the pyre and friends and relatives gather round (B). The priest may be present to recite **mantras** or prayers. The fire is lit and ghee is poured over the wood to ensure that it burns vigorously. One of the prayers asks:

> Dear departed one, may your sight return to the sun and your soul be released to return to the earth to enter a new body or to enter the realms of light.

Later the ashes are gathered up and scattered on the waters of the local river. Many Hindus try to take the ashes to the sacred River Ganges. It is said these holy waters can wash away bad **karma** and help the soul attain

moksha. The Ganges is associated with the god **Shiva** (C) who represents the powers of destruction and death. He is often portrayed as an ascetic deep in meditation and smeared in ashes. He knows the time and place of each person's death and holds the balance of their karma. Hindus approach him with reverence and remember his powers both to destroy all things and to re-create all things.

B 'May your sight return to the sun and your soul be released . . .'

C Shiva dances the rhythm of the Universe, in a circle of flames.

THINGS TO DO

1 Look again at what you have learned about the following Hindu concepts:
   - Brahman
   - Atman
   - Karma
   - Moksha.
   Write a paragraph on the meaning of each of these.

2 Look at Photos A and B. With a partner make a list of the differences between this funeral and any funeral service in the UK. What does this tell you about the Hindu attitude to death and the attitude to death in our society in general?

3 Imagine you are staying in India and you watch a cremation ceremony in the village where you are living. Write a diary page describing what you saw and try to explain what you understand of the ceremony and its meaning.

4 The River Ganges is sacred for all Hindus. Find out more about the traditions surrounding this river. Use the books suggested in the bibliography on page 96 and write up an illustrated article for a magazine on the Ganges and its meaning for Hindus.

5 With a partner list the differences between your own ideas about life and death and the Hindu idea of reincarnation. Discuss your ideas in class.

6 Look at Photo C. What do you think the flames represent? Suggest reasons why Lord Shiva is beating a rhythm on a drum. The circle around him is symbolic; can you guess what it represents? Discuss your ideas and find out more about Shiva.

Judaism: celebrating life

Jews believe that all life is given by God. The **Torah**, the most important of the Jewish scriptures (A), tells of God creating man and woman and breathing life into them. This is described in the stories of the creation in the book of **Genesis**. The chapter ends with the reminder that men and women are not immortal but of the earth: 'you are dust and to dust you shall return'. Life begins and ends according to God's will.

The creation narratives in the Torah offer teachings about life and God's purpose for men and women. According to these stories God intended that people should enjoy and benefit from his creation. They were to be responsible and to look after God's world. They were also to grow in number and to build up the human family on earth.

The Jewish tradition celebrates festivals through the seasons of the year. There are times of joy and feasting and occasions for seriousness and repentance. Through these festivals and special days the Jewish community educates its children and remembers and re-lives important times in the history of the faith. Just as there are seasons and celebrations in the cycle of the year so there are celebrations in the seasons of life.

According to the Jewish tradition human life begins at birth. In the Jewish community the birth of a child is marked with special blessings. When a young person comes of age in the Jewish community the occasion is celebrated with a service at the **synagogue**. Marriage is the beginning of a new season in life and it is marked by the ceremony of the **chuppah**. This is the canopy under which the bride and groom are married and it represents harmony and the new home. In this way the seasons of life are celebrated and given meaning in the Jewish tradition.

Important occasions in the life of the individual are important in the life of the community too. Celebrations and ceremonies bring people together, the community is strengthened and the faith is renewed. The traditions of the community are handed down and the teachings of the faith are put into the context of life.

A   *The Torah being held up in the synagogue.*

Judaism: celebrating life

B   A Jewish family celebrating Sukkat: marking the seasons of the year and of life is important to many people.

THINGS TO DO

1   Look again at the story of Adam and Eve in the book of Genesis. According to Jewish tradition the scriptures are to be interpreted and not just accepted as literal fact. In your interpretation of the story can you find any teaching on the following questions?
   - Why God created human beings.
   - What responsbilities God gave to men and women.
   - Why God created both man and woman.
   - Why men and women shall not live for ever.

2   In the Jewish tradition human life begins at birth. The life of the foetus is important but it is not human life in the same way as after birth. The question of when life actually begins is important. There are many arguments about this. Can you suggest why this is such an important question today? Discuss ideas with a partner and share your thoughts in class.

3   The Hebrew word for 'breath' is the same as the word for 'spirit'. Does this throw light on the story of the creation of Adam in Genesis? What do you think is meant by God breathing life into the body? Discuss this in class.

4   Many Jewish festivals and celebrations involve children.
   - Name the Jewish festivals you know.
   - List the ways in which children are involved in the celebration of these.
   - Suggest reasons why children are so much involved.

5   Some Jews believe that there is an afterlife. Many Jews prefer to say that we cannot know what lies beyond death and we should not waste time pondering the imponderable. Do you think we can know if there is life beyond death or is it better to concentrate on living the life we have now? Discuss this with a partner and open up the topic for a debate in class.

6   There are many ways in which the Jewish tradition makes note of the themes of life and death. Look at and revise the special days and celebrations of the Jewish year. In what ways do these themes appear in the cycle of festivals? Write down your ideas and discuss them in class.

11
The path to holiness

To understand the way in which the life cycle is mapped out and celebrated in the Jewish tradition we need to look at the story of the **Covenant** between God and the people of Israel in the **Torah**. When God promised that Israel would be his people he also gave them the commandment: 'You shall be holy, for I the Lord your God am holy' (Leviticus 19). Every stage and season in life can become an opportunity to try to fulfil this commandment to become holy. There are blessings and prayers for every occasion which serve to remind Jews of God's commandment.

According to Jewish tradition a person has two opposing inclinations: the one towards good and the other towards selfishness. The ceremonies and celebrations in the life of the Jewish community are intended to encourage the inclination towards goodness. In this way the commandment to be holy is continually being fulfilled and worked out through everyday life.

We might ask where we should begin in looking at the life cycle. Should we start with the birth of the child and the beginning of life? Or should we begin with the marriage ceremony – after all, marriage usually comes before the birth of the child. In the first story of creation in Genesis man and woman are told to 'Be fruitful and multiply'. In other words they were commanded to create a family. Having children is thus a way of fulfilling God's purpose.

When a child is born into a Jewish family the words of a blessing are said; for example, when a daughter is born this prayer is said:

> Blessed are You, Lord our God, King of the Universe, who has kept us alive and supported us and brought us to this season.

This blessing is said on all joyous occasions. Birth is an occasion for joy, for celebrating life and the fulfilment of the commandment to be fruitful.

Following the birth of a baby girl the father may be called up at the reading of the Torah in the synagogue to recite the blessings. This is an honour given in **Orthodox** or traditional communities. The baby's name is pronounced in the course of a special prayer. This prayer expresses the hope that she will grow to follow the Torah, find fulfilment in marriage and live a life of good deeds.

A   Procession of the Torah in the synagogue.

B Family life can be a path to holiness in the Jewish tradition.

A Jewish child is given a Hebrew name. The name of a late relative is often taken for the first name. The surname is taken from the father. Every child born of a Jewish mother is Jewish. The status of the individual as a Jew is therefore passed down through the woman. The family identity is given through the father.

C All people are inclined to both good and bad.

THINGS TO DO

1 Look up the texts referred to above: Genesis chapter 1 verses 26–31 and Leviticus chapter 19 verses 1–2. What kind of God comes across in these texts? What does he want? Discuss this in class.

2 Draw a picture or diagram which illustrates the two opposing inclinations in a person – one to do good the other to act selfishly (C). Explain your diagram to a partner and share your ideas. Discuss in what ways you think this picture of human nature is true.

3 A Jewish saying goes: 'As the name is – so is the person who bears it.' Why is a name so important? What does it tell you about a person? Find out the meaning of first names in the class and discuss these questions.

4 In what ways do Jewish families remember and keep God's commandment to be holy? Use the photos to help you.

5 What makes a person's identity? What identity do we start out with? How does that identity grow and develop? Draw a diagram of yourself showing all the things that make up your identity. Discuss your diagram with a partner.

6 What do you understand by the word 'holy'? Write down some of the things you would look for in the life and character, words and actions of someone who was an example of holiness. Discuss your ideas in class.

12
Brit Milah

According to the **Torah** every Jewish boy must be circumcised on the eighth day after he is born. This commandment is recited in the words of the prayer said at the ceremony of **circumcision**:

> Blessed are You, Lord our God, King of the Universe, who makes us holy through doing His commands, and commands us to bring our sons into the Covenant of our father, Abraham.

Brit Milah means the 'Covenant of Cutting'. Circumcision is the cutting and removal of the foreskin on the boy's penis. This simple operation is carried out by a highly trained **mohel** who, in effect, is a surgeon. Some synagogues have a room where circumcisions are carried out and sometimes it is done at the hospital. Circumcision is not often postponed; even if it is **Shabbat** the commandment of circumcision must be kept. Only if the baby is not well or not strong is Brit Milah postponed.

At Brit Milah the father, the trained circumciser and the **sandek** are present. The sandek is a male relative or friend who holds the baby during the ceremony (A). Sometimes a female friend or relative brings the baby into the

B   Brit Milah is a family occasion.

A   Brit Milah: 'Covenant of Cutting'.

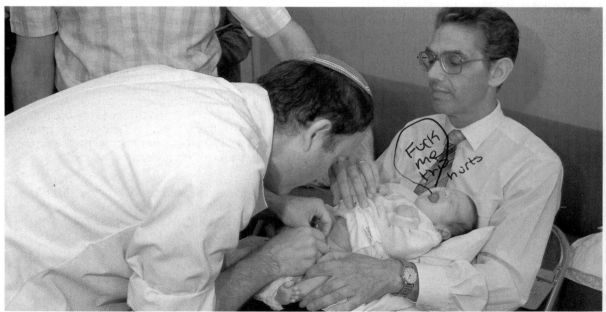

Brit Milah

Circumcision does not make a boy Jewish. He is born Jewish. Nevertheless, circumcision represents a direct link with the first Jew and father of the faith.

Some people have asked why a sign was chosen for men but not for women. It is often argued that women are by nature self-disciplined and more inclined to be religious. It is the men who constantly need reminding of God's commandments and have to be bound to them with the symbol of circumcision.

THINGS TO DO

1 With a partner discuss some possible answers for the following:
- Why is the mother not present at the ceremony?
- Why does the father not hold the child?
- Why is the baby given a taste of wine?
Discuss your answers in class.

2 The ceremony of circumcision links the child with the past in several ways. List the points of connection with the past. Why do you think this plays an important part in the ceremony? Discuss this.

3 Are our roots, our history and background important to us? Draw yourself a diagram or picture showing your roots. It could be a map showing where you have lived, where your parents were from, where you feel most at home, where your grandparents' roots were, where you have spent most of your life, etc.

4 Imagine you have just been to the circumcision ceremony of a cousin. You were either the person who brought in the baby or the one who held him. Write an account of who was there and why the ceremony was important as if you are explaining the ritual and its meaning to someone who is not Jewish.

5 Does life have seasons? What are they? Represent them as a poster and suggest celebrations to mark the seasons of life.

6 Circumcision is a sign of belonging to a group of people and its history. We all belong to a group of some sort: a family or a home or a school, a club or society. What signs of belonging do we have? What responsibilities come with these? Discuss these questions in pairs and share your answers in class.

room. She may take on the role of a sort of 'godparent' while the sandek may become the 'godfather' to the child. This idea of godparents is not general practice. It is a recent introduction to the Brit Milah and some say it has come about through contact with Christian practice. Other members of the family may also be invited. The mother does not attend the ceremony itself, however; she will be present at the festivities afterwards (B).

There is always an empty chair at Brit Milah. This is the chair of **Elijah** who is symbolically present at the ceremony as a witness to the keeping of the Covenant. The father does not hold the child during the ceremony. He recites the blessings. Once the circumcision has been performed someone dips their finger in sweet red wine to give a taste to the baby. Later, relatives and friends are invited for a celebration meal at the family home.

The mark of circumcision is a mark of the Covenant originally made between God and Abraham. It is an outward sign but it is a personal one and this is symbolic of the Covenant requiring a personal response.

13
Bar Mitzvah

Bar Mitzvah means 'Son of the Commandment'. A Jewish boy becomes Bar Mitzvah when he reaches the age of 13 and one day. From that day on he is regarded as an adult in the Jewish tradition.

B The Bar Mitzvah means the Jewish boy is an adult in the religious community, and can read from the Torah in the synagogue.

A Jewish boy at his Bar Mitzvah, with tephilin, tallit and Torah.

Before he becomes Bar Mitzvah the Jewish boy attends classes given by the **rabbi** at the synagogue to prepare him for his new responsibilities as an adult in the Jewish community. He is taught to wear **tephilin** and **tallit** for weekday prayers (A) and he has to study the history of his religion. He learns to recite a passage from the Torah and to understand the meaning of the text. (He will have started to learn the language already during Hebrew classes at the synagogue.) Some children attend Jewish schools where they receive their religious education alongside their formal education and the boys are prepared for Bar Mitzvah in these lessons.

At most synagogues a special service is held to celebrate a boy's Bar Mitzvah. It takes place at the reading of the Torah following his thirteenth birthday. It is a public or congregational service and family and friends are invited. At the point in the service when the Torah is read the boy is called up to the **Bimah** to chant the reading for the day in Hebrew (B). This is considered a great privilege and honour.

When the boy has completed the reading his father says: 'Blessed is he who has released me from responsibility for this child'. From then on it is the boy's own responsibility to follow the teachings of the Torah. He will be able to make up the numbers for worship at the synagogue. (For a full synagogue service there must be ten Jewish men over the age of Bar Mitzvah.) The boy becomes an adult in the eyes of the Jewish community and must take full responsibility for his faith.

Bar Mitzvah

C   Bar Mitzvah is a time for celebrating.

After the ceremony there is a festive meal and celebration (C). Usually the boy receives congratulations and presents from relatives and guests.

THINGS TO DO

1   According to British law a person has the right to take on responsibility for their own religion at 16. Do you think this is too late? Is 13 a better age? Discuss this with a partner and then share your ideas in class.

2   Education is prized in Judaism, especially the study of the Torah. A famous rabbi once said, 'If you have learned much Torah, do not congratulate yourself, for that is why you were created.' What do you think he meant by this? Discuss your ideas in class.

3   Reading the Torah in the synagogue is considered a great privilege. Imagine you are writing your diary the night before your Bar Mitzvah. Describe your thoughts and feelings as you approach the service and become aware of your new reponsibilities.

4   The father of the boy may give a speech at the celebration meal after the service in the synagogue. What do you think a father will want to say on this occasion? He may have something to say to the boy as well as to the guests. Write a short speech a Jewish father might give on the occasion of his son's Bar Mitzvah.

5   The Jewish boy becomes Bar Mitzvah at the age of 13 and a day whether or not he goes through a ceremony at the synagogue. Why do you think many Jewish boys go through the ceremony of reading the Torah? Discuss this in class.

6   Prepare a magazine article on the celebration of Bar Mitzvah in the Jewish tradition. Describe the occasion and say why it is significant. You could include an interview with a rabbi or with a boy who has just become Bar Mitzvah.

14
Bat Mitzvah

The **Bar Mitzvah** ceremony is not mentioned in the Jewish **Torah**. Today's ceremony seems to have developed during the Middle Ages. The ceremony of **Bat Mitzvah** is an even more recent development. Bat Mitzvah means 'Daughter of the Commandment'. The service is celebrated in **Reform** and **Liberal** Jewish communities and takes place at the synagogue. A girl becomes Bat Mitzvah at the age of 12 and the service is usually held on or after the girl's twelfth birthday.

The Bat Mitzvah ceremony is not very different from the Bar Mitzvah service. Sometimes the ceremony is conducted for a group of girls all reaching the age of 12 at about the same time. They read a passage from the scriptures and friends and relatives attend the ceremony. After the service there may be a celebration or party but it is usually not on the same scale as a Bar Mitzvah celebration.

B   Learning the traditions of the faith.

A   Bat Mitzvah: 'Daughter of the Commandment'.

Some young Jewish women have felt that their coming of age is not properly recognized in the Jewish tradition. Others point out that as Jewish tradition indicates that women are not required to keep the same commandments as men, in a sense they are privileged in that they do not have to wear **tephilin** and **tallit**. They do not have to be encouraged to keep the faith in the same way as boys. They are thus acknowledged as being by nature more self-disciplined and inclined to keep God's commandments. All Jews are expected to pray three times a day and are meant to attend services at the synagogue during the week. It is at Shabbat that Jewish women usually attend the synagogue.

Bat Mitzvah

C   Learning to make honey cake for Rosh Hashanah, the Jewish New Year.

Like most Jewish children the girl attends lessons in Hebrew at the synagogue and becomes familiar with the history and tradition of the faith. She receives most of her Jewish education in the home (B) where she learns how to keep the **kosher** food laws and to prepare for Shabbat and festivals (C).

Both Bar Mitzvah and Bat Mitzvah are times for celebration. The coming of age means that the young person is considered fully responsible for keeping the faith and it is no longer anyone else's duty to see that they follow the **Covenant.**

THINGS TO DO

1   What do the photos tell you about growing up in the Jewish faith? What thoughts and feelings, hopes and intentions are expressed in the faces and actions of these people?

2   Imagine you have just been through your Bar or Bat Mitzvah ceremony. You are writing to your best friend who was unable to come to tell them what happened. Give a personal account of how you felt and how things went and what the occasion means for you and for your family.

3   List the differences between Bar Mitzvah and Bat Mitzvah. What do you think accounts for these differences? Discuss the arguments in the text concerning the differences between men and women and share your ideas in class.

4   Design either a Bar Mitzvah or Bat Mitzvah card of congratulations. The usual greeting of congratulations is 'Mazel Tov'. Use symbols from the faith to decorate your card.

5   Invite a Jewish mother to speak to the class about her hopes for her children in bringing them up in the Jewish faith. Ask her to explain what she has to teach her sons and daughters about the faith. Prepare a set of questions to ask in class.

6   Arrange a visit to a synagogue. Ask the rabbi to explain what happens at a Bar Mitzvah ceremony at the synagogue. Find out about the practice concerning Bat Mitzvah in the community.

Marriage in the Jewish tradition

In the Jewish tradition marriage is another occasion on which men and women can seek to become holy as God is holy. The union of man and woman and the creation of a family means they are sharing in the ongoing process of God's creation on earth. Marriage brings joy, security and comfort, and is therefore to be celebrated. It is also to be entered into in all seriousness. Some Jewish couples fast on the day of their wedding until the festivities after the ceremony.

A   A Ketubah: a Jewish marriage contract.

Marriage in the Jewish tradition is an agreement or contract between two people. It is described as 'a convenant of love and companionship, of peace and friendship'. There is a marriage document called the **Ketubah** which sets down the obligations and duties of the husband (A). This is signed by the groom and given as security to the bride. The marriage can only be dissolved by divorce under the Jewish law.

The marriage service usually takes place in the synagogue or at the bride's home. In some **Orthodox** communities the service is held out of doors. In the UK the ceremony takes place in the synagogue. A canopy is set up. It is called the **chuppah** and is a symbol of the harmony and the sanctity of the home the couple will share (B). It is under the chuppah that the couple are brought together. The **rabbi** says a blessing over a cup of wine and the couple take a sip from it twice during the ceremony. The rabbi recites the blessing:

> Blessed are You, Lord our God, King of the Universe, who makes us holy through doing His commands, and who makes His people Israel, holy by the ceremony of the chuppah and the sanctity of marriage.

Marriage in the Jewish tradition

B *Jewish bride and groom under the chuppah.*

The bridegroom puts a ring on the bride's finger and declares, 'You are consecrated to me with this ring according to the faith of Moses and of Israel.' In **Reform** and **Liberal** synagogues the bride may give a ring to the groom in the same way. The Ketubah is read and this is followed by the recital of seven prayers or blessings, such as this one:

Give these, companions in love, great happiness, the happiness of Your creatures in Eden long ago. May Your children be worthy to create a Jewish home, that honours You and honours them. Blessed are You Lord, who rejoices the bridegroom and the bride.

The service ends with the groom breaking the wine glass underfoot. Some say this is a reminder of the destruction of the temple and it adds a note of seriousness amidst the joy.

After the ceremony the couple are given a few moments of privacy before a celebration meal with family and friends. It is traditional for the seven blessings to be sung again and music plays an important part in the festivities.

THINGS TO DO

1 Jewish parents may encourage their sons and daughters to meet people of their own age within the Jewish community. Very occasionally the Jewish community may arrange a meeting if a person expresses a desire to meet a suitable partner. Do you think a community should be involved in this way? What are the advantages of this kind of community concern?

2 Marriage marks the beginning of a new season in a person's life. What changes will it involve? Make a list with a partner and discuss the changes in class.

3 Discuss the meaning of the different symbols in the marriage ceremony. Draw them and write a few sentences to explain their meaning. What symbols are there in other wedding ceremonies? What do they represent? Discuss your ideas in class.

4 Look carefully at Photo B. Imagine you are a member of the bride's family. Write a letter to a relative unable to attend the service describing what happened. Indicate your feelings and hopes for the couple's future. Use words from the service if you wish.

5 In the Jewish tradition the single person is seen as unfortunate. Married life is seen as the best possible life. Is this an understandable point of view? What sort of pressures might this put on people? Discuss this in class.

6 Design an invitation for a Jewish wedding ceremony in a British synagogue. Use one of the blessings or some of the symbols to decorate your invitation.

16

A Jewish funeral

Jewish tradition teaches that it is the duty of everyone to preserve life. Life is a gift from God and other commandments can be put to one side if necessary in order to save life. However, when death comes it is accepted and the response is to acknowledge God's will with the words:

Hear, O Israel, the Lord is our God, the Lord is One. The Lord He is God. The Lord He is God. The Lord He is God.

These words are also said on **Yom Kippur**, the solemn Day of Atonement, when the Jewish community remembers the judgement of God and looks to the future redemption of the world.

Burial is required by the **Orthodox** tradition. The body is to be given the same dignity and respect in death as in life. Some **Liberal** and **Reform** communities allow cremation. The burial should take place within 24 hours of death. The body is washed and wrapped in a white shroud and put into a plain wooden coffin. There are no flowers or wreaths. Family and friends attend the service at the grave. Often women do not attend the funeral service and in Orthodox communities women are encouraged not to. The burial ends with the **Kaddish** which is a prayer recited by members of the close family in praise of God and his goodness.

Immediately after the burial there is a week of solemn mourning for the close family. They stay away from work and are visited by friends and relatives bringing appetizing foods so that they do not have to worry about shopping and cooking. The mirrors in the house are covered. Members of the close family make a small tear in their clothing as a sign of mourning, for example, a man may put a tear in the lapel of his jacket. Soft shoes are worn about the house and a candle of remembrance is lit. For the rest of the month mourning is less intense but it is still respected by friends and relatives.

On the anniversary of the death the family lights a candle in the synagogue and recites the Kaddish which blesses and praises the name of God. This is called the **Yahrzeit**. The anniversary is remembered each year in this way.

Some Jews believe in the resurrection of the dead. Others point out that there are no claims made about life after death in the Torah. It is believed that the body returns to dust and the spirit returns to its source which is God. Some Jews look to a future resurrection in the **Messianic Age** but most believe that these things cannot be known and are best left to God's judgement.

A   Orthodox Jews gathering at a graveyard.

A Jewish funeral

B Yahrzeit candle.

1   In the book of Job in the **Tenakh**, the Jewish Bible, it teaches: 'The Lord giveth, the Lord taketh away; Blessed be the name of the Lord.' Discuss what this means. How will this belief influence a person's attitude to life and to death? Write down your ideas and then discuss them in class.

2   Why do you think that things are kept very simple in the Jewish funeral service? Write a short description of the way in which the Jewish community marks the death of one of its members and indicate the beliefs expressed in the ceremony.

3   Some Jews look to a Messianic Age when the dead will be raised to rule Israel in justice and peace from Jerusalem. Jewish tradition looks forward to God's redemption as well as back to God's help in the past. Do you think it is healthy to look back as well as forward in life? What do you look forward to with hope? What do you look back to as important in your life? Discuss this with a partner and share your views.

4   Signs of mourning are important in many religious communities. Non-religious people sometimes miss the social customs that help people to understand their sadness. Invent two signs or symbols that you think would be helpful ways of telling people that a person is in mourning.

5   Many families name their children after well loved relatives who have died. In this way their name is kept alive and in a sense they live on in the family. In what other ways do people 'live on' after they have died? Discuss this in class.

6   People say it is important to mourn. Find out more about the traditions of mourning in the Jewish tradition. Write a miniproject on them and say what value these rites and rituals may have for the people involved. Use the books in the bibliography on page 96 to help you.

Buddhism: life as an endless cycle

A   An image of the Buddha.

The Buddhist view of life is summed up in the **Four Noble Truths** taught by the **Buddha** (A). The starting point of the Buddha's teaching is that 'All life is suffering' (**dukkha**). Dukkha is an important word in Buddhism. It could be translated in a number of ways. For example, this teaching could be translated as 'All life is unsatisfactory'.

The Buddha taught his followers that the reason we cannot find happiness or satisfaction in life is because we are always wanting things. For example, when we want something and cannot get what we want we are unhappy. On the other hand, when we do get what we want we cannot be really happy because we know it will not last for ever. So this life is unsatisfactory and full of suffering. The answer is to stop the wanting. The problem is that this wanting, or craving, keeps on burning, even after death. It is this craving that brings us back again and again to live many lives on earth.

Buddhists believe, therefore, that this life is only one of many. At death, the flame of life passes on to a new body just as a flame from a dying candle can be used to light a new one. So life continues. There is no soul or self which is passed on, simply a continuous process that leads from one life to the next. There can be no end to this cycle of rebirth unless the wanting or craving is stopped.

According to the teachings of the Buddha, there are three fires that fuel the flame of life. These are ignorance, greed and hatred. These fires must be put out. Then the craving or wanting will stop; but of course it is not easy to stop wanting, to have no desires and no attachments.

B   Buddhist monks in meditation.

Buddhism: life as an endless cycle

The Buddha taught his followers a way to put out the fires of ignorance, greed and hatred. He taught them the **Middle Path**. This leads to **Nibbana** which means 'blowing out'. When followers reach Nibbana they become free from ignorance and greed and from all hatred. There is no flame, no burning desire to bring them back to live again. So they are released from the endless cycle of life, death and rebirth and find eternal peace.

Four Noble Truths

1 Life is unsatisfactory and full of suffering

2 We suffer in this way because we are always wanting

3 The answer to the problem is to stop the craving

4 The way to stop the craving is to follow a 'Middle Path'

Eight Fold, or Middle Path

1 Right Understanding
2 Right Thought
3 Right Speech
4 Right Action
5 Right Livelihood
6 Right Effort
7 Right Mindfulness
8 Right Concentration

THINGS TO DO

1 Look at Photo A. What are the things about this image of the Buddha that tell you:
   - this figure represents an important person
   - this figure represents someone who has found perfect peace
   - this is a religious image?

2 Look again at the Four Noble Truths and the Middle Path. Discuss how it would be possible to overcome the fires of ignorance, greed and hatred.

3 Illustrate the Buddhist teaching 'All life is suffering' with a story which shows that wanting and suffering are closely connected.

4 Look at Photo B. Make a list of all the things in this scene that might tell you that these Buddhist monks no longer desire the things in life that most people want.

5 Wanting things is often what drives us on in life to achieve things. Do you think that it is bad always to want things? What are the things that most people want in life? Why do we want things so much? Discuss these questions with a partner and then share your ideas in class.

6 Represent the three fires of ignorance, greed and hatred using symbols, and design a poster to illustrate and explain how these fires can be put out.

18

Two paths, one way

The Buddhist community is made up of two groups of people. These two groups nourish and support each other. Both groups try to follow the **Dhamma**, the teachings of the Buddha.

On the one hand there is the **Sangha**. This is the community of **bhikkhus** and **bhikkhunis** who share a monastic life. Those who join the Sangha live a life of self-discipline and meditation. Their aim is to reach **Nibbana**. On the other hand there is the Buddhist lay community of people who work, marry, have children and who lead their everyday lives in the usual way.

The lay community treasures the presence of the Sangha and provides the monks and nuns with food and other necessities of life. They may of course visit the Sangha to hear the teachings given there and to join in the **puja** at the shrine of the Buddha. Lay Buddhists hope that in another life they may become monks or nuns and follow the life of the Sangha too. In this life they try to follow the teachings of the Buddha for the lay person. Like the monks and nuns they accept the Three Jewels:

I take refuge in the Buddha
I take refuge in the Dhamma
I take refuge in the Sangha

Every Buddhist also keeps the Five Precepts:

To refrain from taking life
To refrain from taking that which is not given
To refrain from sexual misconduct
To refrain from telling lies
To refrain from taking any kind of drug

Morality, generosity to the Sangha, keeping special days and pilgrimage are all important in the life of those in the lay community.

The way the lay Buddhist should live is set down in the scriptures called **Sigalvada Sutta**. These teachings describe all the social and moral duties for the parent and the child, the teacher and the pupil, the husband and the wife, the employer and the worker. In many countries where Buddhism is the main religious tradition, such as in Sri Lanka, Burma, Thailand, Korea, Tibet and Japan, these teachings play an important part in shaping the life of the community.

There are two main branches of Buddhism, **Theravada** Buddhism and **Mahayana** Buddhism. In Theravadin Buddhist societies it is generally believed that members of the Sangha are closest to Nibbana. Nevertheless,

A   *Buddhist monks and nuns are provided for by the lay community.*

Two paths, one way

B Bodhisatta figure, with hand outstretched to help others.

they do believe that members of the lay community can come closer to Nibbana through leading a good life and gaining a better rebirth.

In the Mahayana tradition there is more emphasis on the idea that it is not only monks and nuns who attain Nibbana. Mahayana Buddhists believe that there are divine beings who offer help to men and women on the path to Nibbana. These saintly helpers are called **Bodhisattas** (B). They are beings who have set aside their own enlightenment in order to help others.

THINGS TO DO

1 Represent two different Buddhist paths in life in a simple diagram, map or chart showing the path of the bhikkhu or bhikkhuni on the way to Nibbana and the path of the lay person who may still have many lives to lead.

2 Buddhist parents, like all parents, want what is best for their children's future. What do you think is the best path in life for a person to follow from the Buddhist point of view? How do you think your parents would react if you were to decide to become a Buddhist monk or nun? Discuss this with a partner and share your ideas in class.

3 Look at Photo A. With a partner discuss what you think is happening in this scene. Write a set of questions you might ask a) the monk, and b) the lay Buddhist in order to find out the meaning of this giving and receiving. Write a set of answers you think might be given to your questions.

4 Look again at the idea of the Bodhisatta. Draw the figure shown in Photo B and write an explanation of the importance of the Bodhisatta in Buddhist tradition.

5 The lay Buddhist tries to keep the Five Precepts. If you had to decide on five simple rules for living what would they be? How do these rules and the Five Precepts compare with other rules for living that you know?

6 Make up a set of teachings to describe employers' responsibilities and duties to their workers and workers' duties and responsibilities to their employers. Do the same for teachers and their pupils. Discuss them in class.

19
Buddhism and popular custom

The **Sangha** relies on the lay community for food and provisions. Without this support and nourishment from the lay community the Sangha could not survive. In return the Sangha provides members of the lay community with spiritual nourishment. The lay Buddhist can attend the Sangha to learn meditation, to hear the teachings of the Buddha given by the monks and nuns and to take part in the **puja** at the shrine. The Sangha also provides the ceremony and ritual that the lay community looks for at certain important times, such as festivals and funerals.

Buddhists see the life of the Buddha as an example to follow and revere him as the embodiment of Truth. The image of the Buddha inspires love and devotion. Gifts of flowers, light, water or incense are offered at his shrine. It is at the shrine at the Sangha that the lay community finds the religious context for marking important occasions such as ceremonies related to death and cremation.

It is significant that there is no Buddhist ritual or ceremony to mark the birth of a child. Families in Buddhist countries usually follow local customs and traditions but these will reflect the 'popular religion' of the area and have little to do with Buddhist beliefs. For example, in some Buddhist countries ancestor worship exists alongside Buddhism and the parents of a new baby may make offerings at the shrines of their family ancestors and pray for them to protect the child and bless him or her with good fortune.

Parents want the best possible start in life for their children. Buddhists believe that a child is not just born for the first time but is re-born

A   Children will learn the story of the Buddha.

Buddhism and popular custom

from a previous existence. This means that there is the possibility that bad influences from a previous life might be carried over into this one. The parents try to bring up the child to follow the teachings of Buddhism so that they can gain merit in future lives (A). In the home the child learns the lessons of loving kindness and compassion from the example of their parents and learns how to offer puja at the shrine of the Buddha.

In the UK, Buddhist Sanghas want to develop contact with the local community (B). Some encourage parents to visit with their children, to join in puja and to learn about how to bring up a child in the Buddhist tradition. A few Sanghas now offer classes for children and provide opportunities for them to hear stories about the Buddha and to learn to meditate.

THINGS TO DO

1 Suggest reasons why there are Buddhist rituals for death and cremation but no ceremony to celebrate birth. Use the information in the last two units to help you think about this question.

2 List the hopes and fears you think most parents have for their child. With a partner discuss some of the practical ways in which a future mother and father might express these hopes and fears.

3 With a partner discuss the ways in which the Buddhist belief about 'being born' is different from your own beliefs. List the questions you would want to ask a Buddhist about their beliefs about birth.

4 Look at Photo B. What do you think children will learn when they attend the Sangha? Design a programme for young children attending Saturday classes at a Sangha in the UK.

5 What do you think are the responsibilities of a good parent? Write an essay on this subject after discussing it in class.

6 Discuss the different ways in which parents try to prepare their children for life. What part does bringing up the child in a religious faith play in this preparation?

B This Buddhist monastery in Cumbria offers classes for children.

Growing up in Buddhist society

Most parents want the best possible education for their children. Many Buddhist Sanghas have always been educational institutions as well as religious communities. They may offer a number of different opportunities for study. For example, some offer part-time language classes in **Pali** or **Sanskrit** for people wanting to study the Buddhist scriptures. Others offer courses on the teachings of the **Dhamma**. In many Buddhist countries there are Sanghas which provide full-time elementary education for children from the lay community. Some also offer full-time secondary education and even higher education. Of course, all Buddhist Sanghas provide classes for those who wish to become monks or nuns.

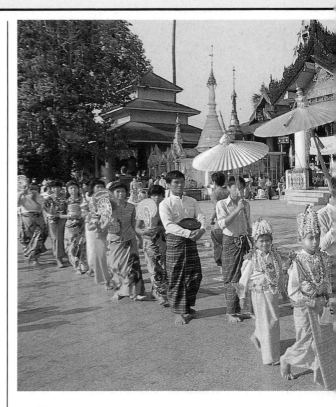

A   A nun supervizes lessons at the Sangha.

When someone wants to become a member of the Sangha they have to go through a ceremony of **Ordination**. There are different levels of Ordination. Higher Ordination is for those who are ready to make a long-term commitment to the life of the Sangha. This is for people who feel ready to become **bhikkhus** or **bhikkhunis** and to devote their lives to the quest for **Nibbana**.

There is another Ordination ceremony which is sometimes called **Initiation** or 'lower Ordination'. This is for lay Buddhists who join the Sangha for a limited period of time and then return to the lay community. Some Sanghas ordain women, although the Initiation ceremony is usually for boys and young men from traditional Buddhist families.

Many Buddhist families send their sons to spend a few months as members of a Sangha in order to receive their religious education and to learn the teaching and example of the Buddha. This time of separation from home and family marks the beginning of a new stage in the young person's life. It may be arranged for the time when the boy has finished his schooling before going to train for a job or profession or before he goes on to higher education. Sending a child to live as a member of the Sangha is believed to bring merit and blessings on the whole family.

Growing up in Buddhist society

B Families may join the procession of the novices to the Sangha.

In the time leading up to Ordination the young person takes lessons from a monk or nun who will prepare him for the vows he will make (A). There are Ten Precepts that he will have to keep at the Sangha.

The Ten Precepts
To refrain from killing or injuring living creatures
To refrain from taking what is not given
To refrain from any sexual activity
To refrain from lying and wrong speech
To refrain from intoxicants
To refrain from eating after midday
To refrain from entertainments
To avoid use of ornaments and perfumes
To refrain from sleeping in a luxury bed
To avoid handling money

There are popular ceremonies associated with the boy's entry into the Sangha. Often the young man is accompanied by a procession of

his family and friends (B). Before he sets out he is dressed in a simple white robe which he will exchange for the saffron robes of the monk at the Sangha. His parents or other relatives will provide him with his robes. The family usually prepares food and provisions for the Sangha.

THINGS TO DO

1 Some people think that time away from home can help a young person to grow up. However, the first time a young person stays away for a long period may be difficult for them. Describe a time when you have been away from home and family or imagine such an event. Describe the things that were worrying or difficult and also the good things about the time you were away.

2 Buddhist Initiation is a rite of passage. A rite of passage is a ritual to mark a change or passage to a new status in life. What other rites of passage can you think of? What do they mean or represent for the people involved and for the community they belong to?

3 Imagine you are a Buddhist parent and you want your son to spend time as a member of the Sangha. Write a conversation between you and your son. You can include other people too if you want to involve another parent, for example, or a brother or sister.

4 Draw or design a poster of the Ten Precepts which a young Buddhist might receive before his or her Ordination.

5 Revise your work on the Buddhist scriptures. Use the books in the bibliography on page 96 to help you. Write 'An Introduction to the Buddhist Scriptures' which would tell someone who didn't know anything about Buddhism something about the scriptures and their teachings.

6 There are many ways in which the Sangha serves the community at large. With a partner draw up a list of the ways you have learned about. Make a poster advertising the activities and opportunities offered at the Sangha.

Initiation

When a young Buddhist sets out to the Sangha for his **Initiation** he may be accompanied by a procession of friends and family. They carry the offerings for the shrine and food for the monks and nuns. In some Buddhist societies the child is dressed in princely clothes before entering the Sangha (A). This is to re-enact the story of the Buddha leaving behind the luxury of the palace to take on the life of a wandering holy man.

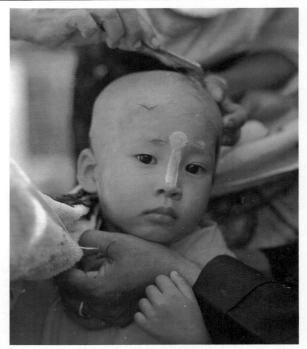

B *Those entering the Sangha must have their heads shaved.*

A *Entering the Sangha: some Sanghas take both boys and girls.*

When the boy arrives at the Sangha he has his head shaved (B). This represents his giving up worldly concerns. It is a mark of poverty and self-discipline. He then presents his saffron robes to the senior monk and bows before him. Kneeling on the floor the boy requests permission to become a member of the Sangha. He vows to keep the rules of the Sangha and to concentrate on overcoming **dukkha**.

The senior monk may then give a short sermon for those entering the Sangha. He may remind them of the teachings of the Buddha. It is important for them to remember that the things of this life cannot bring true happiness because all things pass away and there is nothing permanent to hold on to in this life, not even a soul or self. The aim of the **bhikkhu** is to seek that which lasts for ever and does not perish; this is **Nibbana**.

The boy is dressed in saffron robes with the help of another monk (C). His own teacher then presents him to the senior monk ready for initiation. The boy makes a promise to be obedient to the **Dhamma** and to follow the rules of the Sangha. Once his vows are made he is a member of the community. During his time at the Sangha he receives instruction in the teachings of the Buddha and the practice of meditation. He follows the daily routine of the Sangha which begins before dawn each morning. The bhikkhus and bhikkhunis go out early each day to receive alms from the lay community to provide them with their food for the day. They have a light breakfast and a main meal at midday, and fast after noon.

C   Initiation: receiving saffron robes in the
Sangha.

Sometimes a young Buddhist stays on at the
Sangha, becomes a bhikkhu and dedicates his
life to the quest for Nibbana. Usually he leaves
to take up his place in society, to train for a job
or profession or to enter higher education.
Later he will marry and start a family of his
own.

THINGS TO DO

1   Look at Photos A, B and C. With a partner
discuss what is happening in these scenes.
Write a commentary of the events.

2   The life of the Sangha is simple and ordered.
Why do you think this is? What would you find
most difficult about this life? Is there anything
about it that you might find helpful or
challenging? What might be learned from it?
Discuss these questions in class.

3   Bring in photos of yourself. Look at changes
in yourself from the time when you were a
toddler. Look at changes in the last few
years. What remains unchanged? What is left
of the old you? Is there any part of you that is
permanent and unchanging? Is there such a
thing as a self or soul? Discuss these
questions and decide whether there is some
truth in the Buddhist teaching that there is no
individual self or soul.

4   Imagine you have just entered the Sangha
and have been away from home for a few
days. Write a letter to your family describing
your life as a member of the Sangha, the
things you are learning and how you feel
about the kind of life you are living there.

5   With a partner list all the facilities a Sangha
needs. Design a ground plan to show things
like the library, shrine room, etc. and explain
the design in writing.

6   Meditation is an important part of the life of
the Sangha. Find out more about Buddhist
meditation. Invite a Buddhist to come and
explain about Buddhist meditation to the
class. Prepare a set of questions to ask.

Buddhism and marriage

Bhikkhus and **bhikkhunis** do not marry. Sometimes a person who has been married may become a member of the Sangha later in life when they have fulfilled all their family responsibilities. Marriage is for the lay community.

Buddhists consider marriage and family life to be very important. It is believed that these things bring balance and stability to society. However, there is no Buddhist marriage ceremony or ritual for a wedding. Usually the

B   A Buddhist bride and groom in Thailand.

traditions and customs of the local culture are followed. For example, in the UK, a Buddhist couple will marry at the **register office**. Some Sanghas are finding that they get requests from Buddhist couples for a ceremony of blessing after their register office wedding. This is not a marriage ceremony, as the couple are already married, but it may give the occasion special meaning in a way that the register office cannot.

On such an occasion the Sangha may invite the couple to attend **puja** at the shrine of the Buddha. There may also be a sermon from one of the monks on the responsibilities which the couple have for one another according to Buddhism. Buddhist tradition recognizes the woman as an equal partner in the marriage relationship and the teachings of the Buddha emphasize the importance of her status in the community. Both husband and wife must seek to follow the teachings of the Buddha in married life. They must accept the Three Jewels, keep the Five Precepts and bring up their children to know and follow the teachings of the Buddha.

A   A Buddhist bride and groom. Marriage is important in the lay community.

Buddhism and marriage

C   *A Buddhist shrine at the Sangha*

At the blessing of the marriage at the Sangha the families involved bring gifts of food and prepare a meal for the bhikkhus and bhikkhunis and everyone may join in the shared meal after the ceremony. The couple will return with further gifts for the Sangha on future occasions.

The daily life of the lay Buddhist is concerned with work, with earning a living and with bringing up a family. It is too full of cares and worldly desires to lead to the peace of **Nibbana**. Lay Buddhists know that they will have to wait until another life before they can follow the path that leads to Nibbana. However, if they fulfil their duties and follow the teachings of the Five Precepts they can be reborn into a better life and progress one step further towards the journey to Nibbana.

THINGS TO DO

1   Those who become members of the Sangha give up married life and all its advantages and comforts. Do you think that this is a lot to give up? What rewards do you think the bhikkhu or bhikkhuni receives instead of rewards of marriage? Discuss this in class.

2   Many couples who have a register office wedding feel they want a religious ceremony to follow, such as a service of blessing. Why do you think this is? Discuss this with a partner and share your ideas in class.

3   Design a wedding ceremony for a couple who are not religious but who want their marriage to be meaningful, memorable and special. You can choose readings, poems and music, and invent symbols for the occasion.

4   Imagine that you have chosen to give up the path of work, marriage and family life in order to become a monk or nun. Write a letter to a friend explaining what you have chosen to do and why.

5   Imagine you have met someone you want to marry. He or she is a Buddhist. What difference would this make to your future life together? Would you be willing to have a blessing at the Sangha after the wedding? What difficulties might such a marriage bring with it and what benefits too?

6   Why do you think there is no Buddhist marriage ceremony? What does this tell you about the nature of Buddhism? Discuss this in your class.

23
Death rites in Buddhism

A *A cremation procession showing the highly decorated coffin: in some communities the preparations are very elaborate.*

Death rites in Buddhism

According to the teachings of Buddhism, death is not to be feared by those who follow the Middle Path. Death is only a stepping stone in the journey towards **Nibbana**. When a lay person has tried to follow the teachings of the Buddha, accepting the Three Jewels and keeping the Five Precepts faithfully, then death brings with it the promise of a better rebirth which will bring them one step closer to Nibbana. So death is not to be feared.

For those who have followed the life of the **bhikkhu** or **bhikkhuni** and who have reached enlightenment then death is positively to be welcomed. Death will mean the attainment of Nibbana. It will mean the end of suffering and release from the cycle of rebirth. When we look at these beliefs it is not surprising to find that Buddhist ceremonies for the dead are not usually occasions of great mourning or for showing excessive grief.

When someone dies in the Buddhist community, the body is washed carefully. It is laid in a wooden coffin and adorned with flowers. The coffin is carried in a procession to the local Sangha or temple shrine. Gifts of food are taken for the monks and nuns and offerings of flowers are prepared for **puja** at the shrine. Rituals vary from one place to another. In some communities, the coffin is set down in a prominent position and surrounded by all the flowers and gifts brought by family and friends. The monks and nuns lead the gathering in puja and there may be a sermon on the teachings of the Buddha on death and rebirth. Then the family prepare food and offer it to the monks and nuns. Family and friends share a meal together. The ceremony may give the impression of being more like a festival than a funeral. Friends and relatives greet each other and signs of grief are not displayed. The bereaved hope that the deceased will be reborn in a better life and progress on the journey to Nibbana.

The body is later cremated and the ashes collected. Usually they are scattered into the waters of a lake or river or into the sea.

THINGS TO DO

1 Do we sometimes talk about death as a 'release'? What is meant by this? Is death necessarily a bad thing? Discuss these questions in class. Write a poem, play or story in which death is seen as a release or a good, positive thing.

2 Invite a member of the Buddhist community to talk to the class about the Buddhist approach to death.

3 Look at Photo A. Say what is happening in this scene. Imagine you are present at this Buddhist funeral. Write a magazine article on 'Death Rites in Buddhism'.

4 What do you think is the best way for a community or family to mark the death of a loved one? Discuss your ideas with a partner. Write a description of the things you think would be important on such an occasion.

5 In our society black is worn as a sign of mourning. In many cultures the colour is white. Why do you think that colours are important symbols at such times as death and at funeral ceremonies? Find out more about the mourning traditions of different cultures and religions. Use the books in the bibliography on page 96 to help you.

6 Some people say it would be good to live for ever. Do you think this is true? What would be the disadvantages of living for ever? What do you think is attractive about the idea? Discuss this in a group then share your ideas in class.

Christianity: the journey of life

Many Christians see life as being like a journey. This journey is an opportunity to learn and to grow in faith. Christians believe that God guides and supports them on this journey as a parent looks after a child. Like most long journeys life has times of joy and times of sorrow or difficulty. There are also turning points and milestones on the way. There are many Christian churches and traditions. Each has its own way of marking and celebrating the stages in the journey of life.

The Christian journey in life is one of following in the footsteps of Jesus **Christ**. Christians believe that Jesus' life was an example for them to follow. Jesus spent much time in prayer and showed compassion to the outcast, the needy and the sick. This is not an easy path to follow and Christians know that they need to renew their commitment to Christ's teaching over and over again. Some of the most important turning points in life are occasions for believers to think about their faith and make a new beginning.

Christians speak of life as a gift from God. It is therefore something precious and to be treasured. According to the teachings of the **Bible** the gift of life carries with it an important responsibility. Each person should develop the strengths, abilities and talents they have been given and put them to good use. The birth of a baby is a time of great hope and promise. Christians believe that it is a time to thank God for the new life and to prepare the way for the child as it starts out on its own journey in life.

Many Christians feel that the best way to do this is to bring the new baby into the membership of their church. In this way the child will belong to a caring and supporting community right from the beginning. To celebrate the arrival of a new baby and the child's entry into the community many churches have a service of **Infant Baptism**. Some churches call this a **Christening**. At a Christening the child is named and welcomed as a member into the Church.

A *What things do you think will help the Christian in the journey of life?*

B   *Orthodox Christening.*

There are many Christians who like to have their children Christened while they are still small babies. In the Russian **Orthodox** Church, for example, the child is baptized within eight days of birth. The church is lit with candlelight. The priest fills the **font** with water. The font is the bowl or container used especially for Baptism. He blesses or consecrates the water. With this water he baptizes the child and makes the mark of the cross on the forehead. The child is given its Christian name and is welcomed into the church community.

THINGS TO DO

1   There is a famous book called *A Pilgrim's Progress* which tells the story of the Christian's journey in life. What things do you think will help a Christian to progress on this journey. Use picture A to help you.

2   Draw your own map called 'A pilgrim's progress.'

3   Design a questionnaire to find out how people view life, e.g. do they see it as a journey or a cycle? Do they think it leads anywhere? For homework get three people to answer your questions. Discuss your findings in class.

4   Look at Photo B. What are the symbols you can identify in this service and what do you think they stand for in Baptism? Work on the answers with a partner and discuss them in class.

5   What gifts and talents can a person have? Do you think it is wrong to let these things go to waste or does it not matter? Discuss this in pairs and then share your ideas in class.

6   Birth is a time of hope and promise for the future. What hopes and plans do you think the parents of a new-born baby have? Write your ideas in a poem, play or story.

Infant Baptism

There are different services for **Baptism** in different churches. The **Anglican** service of **Infant Baptism** is called a **Christening**. It usually takes place during the regular Sunday service. **Godparents** are chosen by the parents of the child and are invited to the service. They have a special responsibility to keep in touch with the child and to care about his or her religious and spiritual upbringing.

At the service the parents and godparents stand at the **font** with the vicar (A). Usually the mother or father holds the baby. The water in the font is **consecrated**. The vicar recites prayers of thanksgiving for the new life of the child. He reminds the parents and the godparents of their own commitment and duty to Christ. The parents are asked to name the child and the vicar takes the baby in his arms and repeats the name. He lifts a little water on to the child's forehead saying 'I baptize you in the name of the Father, the Son and the **Holy Spirit** (B). The vicar then makes the sign of the cross on the child's forehead saying 'I sign you with the sign of the cross, the sign of Christ'. The parents and godparents are sometimes given a candle to hold. They are asked to confirm their belief in God and their commitment as Christians. They promise to bring up the child in the faith.

Like the Anglican Church, **Roman Catholic** tradition has an Infant Baptism ceremony at which parents and godparents make promises on behalf of the child. After an Infant Baptism there is often a family celebration at home with all the relatives and friends who came to the service. In some households special

A *Christening in an Anglican family. Can you identify the people present?*

Infant Baptism

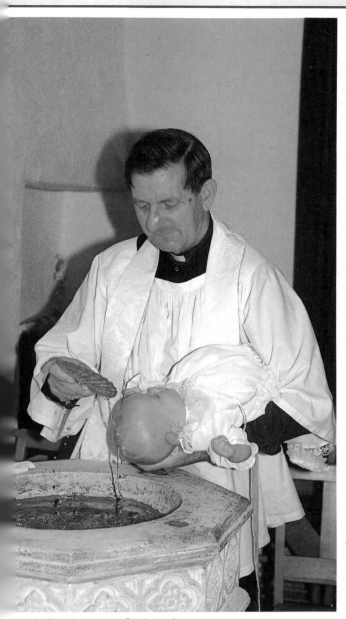

B   Anglican Christening.

Christening cake is served. The godparents and relatives may give a Christening present to the baby to mark the occasion.

Some Christians choose to have a simple **Dedication** rather than a Christening or Infant Baptism for their child. A Dedication service celebrates the birth of the baby and the infant is given their Christian name but is not baptized. The parents promise to bring up the child in the Christian faith. Later the child may be baptized when he or she is old enough to understand the meaning of Christian commitment.

THINGS TO DO

1   In old churches the font is at the entrance of the church to symbolize the child's entry into the Christian faith. Today the font is usually at the front of the church near the lectern and pulpit. Discuss why this has changed. Draw an example of a font – perhaps you can visit a local church and draw the font there. Write an explanation of the place and purpose of a font.

2   Birth is a time for celebration but also a time when people find they have to make big changes in their lives. What changes take place in a family when a child is born for:
   ● mother
   ● father
   ● other children
   ● grandparents?
   Discuss this in class.

3   Look at Photos A and B. What symbols and symbolism are at work in the ceremony? With a partner list the different symbols and try to work out what they stand for. Discuss them in class.

4   Design a card a Christian godparent might send at a Christening or Infant Baptism. Use some of the symbols you listed in Question 3 in your design. Write a message to the mother and father expressing your congratulations and hopes for the child's future.

5   Imagine you are the older brother or sister of the child being baptized in a Christening or Infant Baptism ceremony. Write up a diary for the day describing what happened and express your thoughts and feelings on the day.

6   Invite your local vicar to describe the Christening or service of Infant Baptism as it is celebrated in his church. Make a list of questions in class that you might ask him.

26

Growing in the faith

In many churches there is a special service when bread and wine are shared in remembrance of the **Last Supper**. This service is called by different names in different churches: **Mass**, **Holy Communion**, the **Lord's Supper** and the **Eucharist**.

In the Roman Catholic and Anglican Churches the Mass or Eucharist is the main expression of Christian worship. Young children are not given the bread and wine. Taking Communion or Mass, or sharing the **Breaking of Bread** for the first time is considered an important step in the Christian's journey of faith.

In the Roman Catholic tradition there is a special service when children take their first Communion. They prepare for Mass by learning to say sorry to God for the things they have done wrong. This is called **confession**. In the Roman Catholic tradition, sometimes the

A   Blessing the bread and wine.

person will ask the priest to hear his or her confession. Usually a Christian makes a personal confession in their private prayers before the Mass.

On the day of their first Communion (B) the children usually wear their best clothes, often made or bought for the occasion. The priest invites them to come up to the altar to receive the **host** with the rest of the congregation. The host is the wafer representing the bread of the Last Supper and is believed by Catholics to be the body of Christ. When they receive the host Christians remember Jesus' death on the cross

and the forgiveness of sins which he promised his followers.

In some churches there is no special service to mark the first time a person shares the bread and wine. In the Baptist Church people are invited to share in the Breaking of Bread or Lord's Supper whenever they feel they are ready to do so. In the Anglican Church people do not take Communion until they have been confirmed.

B *Christians in Panama receiving their first Holy Communion.*

THINGS TO DO

1 Look again at the different services which celebrate the Last Supper. List all the names for the service. Draw out the similarities and differences between the various traditions.

2 Design a greetings card that a Catholic child might receive on the occasion of their first Communion. Write an appropriate message inside that the godparent might send.

3 Invite a Roman Catholic priest to speak to the class about the meaning of the Mass in the Catholic tradition. Ask him to explain the way in which Catholics see the journey of life.

4 Look at Photo B. Imagine you are present at the service. Describe what is happening and explain the meaning of the event as if it is your younger brother or sister taking their first Communion.

5 Sharing food is an important symbol in religious tradition. With a partner list all the shared meals and symbols of food you know of in the different religions and jot down what the meaning is behind each ceremony.

6 Times of saying sorry to God for things they have done wrong are an important part of Christians' onward journey in the faith. Why do you think this is? Why is saying sorry so important? Discuss these questions in class.

Confirmation

Confirmation is an important turning point in the life of a Christian in the Anglican and Roman Catholic traditions. The traditions vary from one Church to another but the meaning is the same. To confirm means 'to make firm'. When a child is baptized as a baby the **godparents** and parents promise to ensure the child grows up in the Christian faith. At Confirmation the Christian makes firm his or her commitment to follow Christ and takes on the responsibility for their own faith. Christians believe that God's power and presence is known through the work of the **Holy Spirit**. At Confirmation Christians are reminded that the Holy Spirit can work through them and strengthen their faith.

The person being confirmed usually attends Confirmation lessons (A). These are taken by the vicar or his assistant. At Confirmation classes Christians learn to take their religion more seriously through regular prayer, Bible reading and service in the community. They learn about the Church and the meaning of Communion. Before the Confirmation service there is usually a practice at the church.

Confirmation is performed by a **bishop**. At the Anglican Confirmation service Christians declare their personal faith by answering these questions:

'Do you turn to Christ?'
'Do you repent of your sins?'
'Do you renounce evil?'

A   These young people are studying in preparation for their Confirmation.

Confirmation

words to the newly confirmed Christians on the meaning of their promises and new commitments. Sometimes the Confirmation service is followed by a celebration of the **Eucharist** and the newly confirmed take their first Holy Communion. When the Confirmation is over the family may invite godparents, close friends and family to the house for some refreshment. Sometimes the young Christians receive presents from their godparents to mark the occasion.

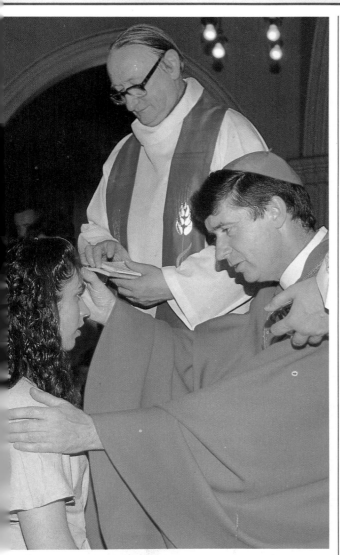

B   Roman Catholic Confirmation. Traditions vary from one church to another

The bishop then asks three further declarations of commitment:

'Do you believe and trust in God the Father who made the world?'
'Do you believe and trust in his Son, Jesus Christ, who redeemed mankind?'
'Do you believe and trust in his Holy Spirit who gives life to the people of God?'

The Confirmation candidates declare their faith and kneel before the bishop (B). He places his hands on the head of each one and says 'Confirm, O Lord, your servant – with your Holy Spirit'. Each one replies 'Amen'.

The service includes hymns, prayers and a reading from the Bible. The bishop says a few

THINGS TO DO

1   Confirmation is a serious step for a Christian. Write down the things a young Christian might want to ask their vicar or priest before getting confirmed. What questions do you think the vicar will ask? Work on these with a partner and read them in class.

2   Invite your local vicar or priest to explain how he prepares young people for Confirmation and to describe what happens at the service. Prepare a set of class questions for him.

3   Look at the photos. How can you tell that this is an important occasion for a) the young person being confirmed and b) the Christian community? Is this an important occasion for anyone else? Why do you think the godparents are usually invited to the service? Discuss these questions in class.

4   Invite a confirmed Christian to talk to the class about their Confirmation and what it means for them. Imagine you are an Anglican Christian. You have just been confirmed. Write up your diary page for that evening. Describe how and why the service was important for you.

5   Design a service sheet for the congregation at a Confirmation service in an Anglican church. Choose a reading from the New Testament. Take 'The Holy Spirit' as your theme. Find a hymn you think might be suitable. The Lord's Prayer should have a place too. Make up some prayers that might be appropriate.

6   Sometimes a young Christian does not feel ready for Confirmation. Some parents may be disappointed by this. Act out a conversation in which this situation is discussed.

28

Believer's Baptism

In some churches, such as the Baptist Church, there is no Infant Baptism or Christening. This is because the community believes it is better to wait until the person is old enough to take a personal responsibility for their faith. In these churches there is a service called **Believer's Baptism**. This is an important step marking the Christian's readiness to make a full personal commitment to the faith.

In a Baptist church there is a pool called the **baptistry**. This is filled with water for Believer's Baptism. It is kept empty and covered up when not in use. The baptistry is usually at the front of the church.

Christians look to the baptism of Jesus as the origin of the rite of baptism in the Church. The Christian Bible says that Jesus commanded his disciples to baptize believers. Baptism is a symbol of the start of a new life as a follower of Christ.

Believer's Baptism today may celebrate the occasion when a person has newly converted to Christianity and wants to express their intention to live a new life. It may mark the time when a Christian feels ready to make a full and personal commitment to the faith in which they were brought up. Before a believer is baptized they normally attend preparation classes. These are taken by the minister. Those being baptized learn about the meaning of baptism and have an opportunity to ask questions about the faith.

The service of Believer's Baptism is usually held during the regular Sunday service. The baptistry is filled beforehand. The minister chooses the Bible readings and theme of his sermon to suit the occasion. In some churches those being baptized make a public declaration of their faith and commitment before they step down into the water. When standing in the water the minister asks the believer to answer the question: 'Do you confess Jesus Christ as your Saviour and Lord?' The believer says 'I do'. The minister then says 'On your confession of faith in Jesus Christ as Saviour and Lord, I

A   Standing in the baptistry.

B   'I baptize you'

C Jesus was baptized in the River Jordan and some churches hold their Believers' Baptisms outdoors.

baptize you in the name of the Father, the Son and the Holy Spirit'. Then he supports the believer, lowers them under the water and lifts them again. Afterwards hymns are sung and those who have been baptized go to dry themselves and change into dry clothes.

Believer's Baptism requires total immersion under the water. This is symbolic of dying and rising again with Christ. Christians say it also represents the washing away of sin. Sometimes after baptism there follows a celebration of **Breaking of Bread** at which the **Last Supper** is remembered.

THINGS TO DO

1 The photos in this unit show parts of the baptism service. In pairs discuss what is happening in each one and try to identify the stages of the ceremony. Write a commentary.

2 Look up the story of the baptism of Jesus in the Gospel of Matthew chapter 3 verses 1–17. Look, too, at the commandment to the disciples to baptize in Matthew chapter 28 verses 1–20. Discuss the stories and what they might say to Christians today.

3 Imagine you are present at a Believer's Baptism service at which a friend of yours is baptized. Write up an account of what happened and what the event meant to your friend.

4 Christians believe that faith in Christ should express itself in a new life. What sort of life do you think that might be? With a partner discuss a list of characteristics that such a life might have.

5 In the Baptist Church there is neither Infant Baptism service nor Confirmation ceremony. Why do you think this is? Write down three reasons and discuss them in class.

6 Invite a Baptist to visit the class. Ask them to explain why they have Believer's Baptism rather than Infant Baptism. Write a list of questions to ask about Believer's Baptism.

Christian marriage

The different churches have different marriage services yet they express the same beliefs. Christians believe that marriage is the union of two people in a faithful relationship of love and companionship for life. Christians believe that this union is brought about by God. The Christian marriage ceremony is therefore both a serious occasion and a joyful one.

Before marrying a couple in church the vicar, minister or priest spends some time with the couple discussing the meaning of Christian marriage. He explains the vows they will make and takes them through the steps of the ceremony.

At the wedding ceremony in an Anglican church, the bride and groom stand facing the vicar at the altar. The groom has his best man on his right. To begin the service the vicar reminds everyone present that: 'We have come together in the presence of God, to witness the marriage of — and to ask his blessing on them and to share their joy. . . . The scriptures teach us that marriage is a gift of God in creation and a means of his grace, a holy mystery in which man and woman become one flesh.'

The vicar explains that marriage is an opportunity for the couple to grow in each other's love and to enjoy each other's companionship, to have a family and to begin a new life together as husband and wife in the community. Prayers are said asking for the couple to be strengthened and guided by God.

The vicar asks if anyone knows of any lawful reason why the couple should not be joined in marriage. Then he reminds the couple of the seriousness of the vows they are going to make and asks the congregation to stand. The vicar names the groom and asks the groom, '—, will you take — to be your wife? Will you love her, comfort her, honour and protect her and, forsaking all others, be faithful to her as long as you both shall live?' The groom answers, 'I will.' The vicar names the bride and says, '—, will you take — to be your husband? Will you

A Bride and groom facing the altar at an Anglican wedding.

Christian marriage

love him, comfort him, honour and protect him and, forsaking all others, be faithful to him as long as you both shall live?' The bride says, 'I will.' Then the bride and groom are each asked to recite the words of the well known vow: 'I take you, —, to be my husband/wife, to have and to hold from this day forward; for better, for worse, for richer for poorer, in sickness and in health, to love and to cherish, till death us do part, according to God's holy law; and this is my solemn vow.'

The best man passes the ring to the vicar who gives it to the groom to put on the bride's finger; in some services, the bride may also put a ring on the groom's finger. The bride and groom are then declared to be man and wife and the vicar says 'That which God has joined together let no man divide.'

There is usually a hymn and a Bible reading and the vicar gives a brief sermon. At the end of the service the couple go to sign the marriage register required by law to record the marriage. After the service there is a festive meal with friends and families to celebrate the occasion.

THINGS TO DO

1 Look at the words of the church marriage service. With a partner write down all the beliefs regarding marriage you can find expressed in the words of the service.

B Orthodox Christian wedding.

2 In a Bible look up St Paul's First Letter to the Corinthians chapter 13. Read it through. Do you think that St Paul has said all there is to say about love? What would you want to add? Why do you think this reading is popular at wedding ceremonies? Discuss these questions in class.

3 What do you think a vicar will want to explain to a couple about Christian marriage? Write a short sermon he might give which explains the meaning of Christian marriage and which is addressed to the couple getting married in church.

4 Look at Photo B; find out how marriages are celebrated in other Christian denominations such as the **Orthodox** tradition, which has a much longer service than the Anglican one . Use the books in the bibliography on page 96 to help you, or invite someone from another church to come and speak to the class.

5 Many couples who are not practising Christians still want to marry in a church rather than in a **register office**. With a partner list the possible reasons for this. Should the Church encourage this? Discuss your answers in class.

6 The Christian Bible and the marriage service talk about a couple becoming 'one flesh' when they marry. What do you think this means? Discuss it with a partner and share ideas in class.

Death

According to the Christian Bible, the **Resurrection** of Christ was a sign that he had overcome the power of death. This leads many Christians to believe that death is not the end. Some Christians believe that the body dies but the person will be raised in a spiritual body. Other Christians believe that after death the **soul** is reunited with God and finds eternal peace.

At the death of a friend or relative people want to express their sadness and have an opportunity to show their respect and love for the person who has died. The different Christian churches have different services to mark the occasion of death. In some, such as the **Orthodox** Church, the funeral ceremony and rites of mourning are elaborate and full of symbolism. This helps the bereaved to come to terms with the death of the loved one and to learn from the grief and loss.

The Christian tradition allows burial or cremation. At a cremation the vicar, minister or priest from the church of the dead person meets the family and friends at the local crematorium. Close relatives arrange for an undertaker to see to the preparation of the body for cremation. The body is washed and laid out in a coffin which is taken to the chapel at the crematorium. The service is fairly short and includes prayers for the soul of the departed, Bible readings and sometimes a hymn too. In the Roman Catholic tradition the funeral service always begins with the celebration of **Mass**, whether it is at the crematorium or church. Later the ashes are collected and taken to the graveyard for burial or are scattered in the 'Garden of Rest', at the crematorium.

A   Christian cremation.

Death

B   Christian burial.

service the vicar, minister or priest says a blessing before the mourners leave the graveside. The service may vary from one church to another. Nevertheless, the message is the same, and that is the promise of God's love which is stronger than death itself.

THINGS TO DO

1   People say that a funeral service is not for the person who has died but for the people they have left behind. Is this true? In what ways will a service help the mourners? Discuss these questions with a partner. Write up your ideas.

2   Most Christians would agree that they don't know exactly what happens after death. Read the teaching of St Paul in his First Letter to the Corinthians chapter 15 and discuss what he is saying about life after death.

3   Mourning is an important process for those who have lost loved ones. There are many things to come to terms with. With a partner try to make a list of the changes, feelings and thoughts the bereaved person may have to cope with. Discuss ways in which the bereaved person might be helped in coming to terms with the loss of someone close.

4   Find out about the funeral and mourning rites in the Christian **Orthodox** tradition. Use the bibliography on page 96 to help you.

5   Sometimes a priest or vicar may visit a dying person to pray with and for them and to offer words of comfort from the scriptures. How can a person prepare for death? What things might be important for them at this time? Discuss this with a partner and write down your ideas.

6   Invite a vicar or priest to speak to the class about:
   • the practice of visiting the dying
   • funeral rites at his church.
   Prepare a set of questions to ask him.

At a Christian burial the coffin is usually carried to the church or graveyard. The service may begin in the church with a reading, hymn and prayers before the coffin is taken out to be buried. The vicar, minister or priest reminds the congregation of the promise of the Resurrection and the everlasting love of God which is stronger than death. The coffin is lowered into the ground and the family stand near the grave while the vicar scatters some soil on to the top of the coffin saying, 'We commit the body to the ground, earth to earth, ashes to ashes, dust to dust.' At the close of the

Islam: freedom to choose

Muslims believe that **Allāh** (God) is the giver of all life – not only the life we have now but also life after death. This is explained in the teachings of their holy book, the **Qur'ān**:

> 'How is it that you do not believe in Allah? since you were dead, and he gave you life; he will hereafter cause you to die, and will again restore you to life; then shall you return unto him.' (Chapter 2)

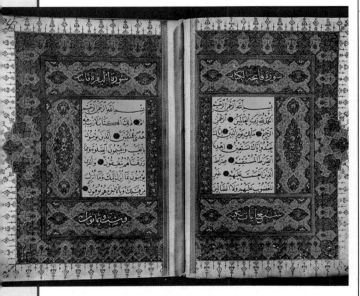

A   *The opening pages of the Muslim holy book, the Qur'ān.*

This life is a gift and with this gift comes the freedom to choose how to live. Muslims believe that Allāh gives everyone the choice to live as they wish. A person can follow their own desires and live a self-centred existence or they can follow the will of Allāh and live a God-centred life. Islam means submission and Muslims are men and women who submit to the will of Allāh.

There is no baptism and no special ceremony by which a person becomes a Muslim or confirms their faith in Islam. Someone who submits to the will of Allāh is a Muslim and this submission is expressed in a simple declaration of belief and in the way the person lives their life. Muslims declare their faith by the words: 'There is no God but Allāh and **Muhammad** is Allāh's Messenger.'

This statement of faith is the **Shahadah**, the first of the **Five Pillars** of Islam. The other four pillars are: **Salah** or prayer, **Zakāh** or giving to the poor, **Saum** or fasting during the month of **Ramadān** and lastly **Hajj** or pilgrimage to **Makkah**.

The act of prayer five times a day gives shape and structure to the daily life of Muslims. The fast in the month of Ramadān gives a focus and structure to the Muslim year. Every Muslim tries to go on the Hajj at least once in their lifetime. This pilgrimage is the highpoint in the life of the devout Muslim. In this way the day, the year and the lifetime of the Muslim are given shape and meaning by acts of submission and devotion to Allāh.

Islam: freedom to choose

B   *Salah is one of the Five Pillars of Islam.*

THINGS TO DO

1   Do we have a choice about the way we live our lives? At what stage in life do we have the choice to live as we wish? Can we do anything we want when we are adults? Discuss these points in a small group and then share your ideas in class.

2   Revise what you have learned about the Five Pillars. Write about two of these explaining the way in which they express submission to Allāh and how they shape and guide the life of Muslims.

3   Many religions speak of life as a gift. What do you think they mean? Does it mean that life is a good thing? Some people might say that life is a burden. What might a religious believer say to them? Discuss these issues in class.

4   Design a poster or diagram that shows the two possible paths in life according to Muslims, i.e. the way that is self-centred and the way of submission to Allāh.

5   Some people argue that it is best not to bring up a child in a religion but to let them choose later when they are old enough. Is this a good idea? Is there then any real choice on offer? What arguments can be put against this suggestion? Organize a class debate on this question.

6   Muhammad said, 'There are two blessings which most people misuse – health and leisure'. What do you think he meant? What other gifts in life do people misuse? How can we make sure that we do not misuse the gifts of life? Write your thoughts on these questions and discuss them in class.

C   *Hajj, the pilgrimage to Makkah, is the last of the Five Pillars.*

32

Birth and naming

Muslims believe that the gift of life is very precious. The birth of a baby is therefore an occasion of great joy and thanksgiving. Muslim parents feel that to be able to bring children into the world and to raise them to be Muslims is both a great responsibility and a great privilege. Children are nurtured in the Muslim faith from their earliest moments.

Soon after the birth of a child, the father or any member of the family, or the local **imām**, is required to whisper the words of the **Adhān** into the right ear of the baby. The Adhān is the Muslim call to prayer. It begins with the words: 'God is greatest' or 'Allāhu Akbar'. This call to prayer is repeated four times in the right ear. Then the words of the **Iqamah** are repeated in the baby's left ear (A). The Iqamah is similar to the Adhān. Lastly the words 'There is no god but Allāh' are recited. This, of course, usually takes place in the hospital. It cannot really be called a ceremony. Although important, it is not seen as an initiation into Islam because a person can only be a Muslim of their own free will.

Several days after the birth there is a ceremony held at the home of the child's parents. This is called the **Aqiqah**. Friends and relatives are invited. The baby's head is shaved of its fine hair as a symbol of purification. Traditionally on this occasion parents gave the weight of the hair in gold or silver to charity.

The Aqiqah is marked by the making of a **sacrifice**. In the case of a boy, two sheep are bought and sacrificed and for a girl, one. The meat is prepared by the **halāl** butcher and divided into three portions. One is kept for the family. Another is for the friends and relatives and is usually prepared as a meal for after the ceremony. The third portion is given to the poor and needy. In this way the family share their good fortune and happiness with others.

The naming of the child takes place on this occasion. The name is usually chosen by the parents but in some cases the most senior member of the family decides on it. The name for a baby boy is taken from the names in the **Qur'ān** and is often a name of one of the **prophets**. It is chosen for its meaning. A girl's name may also be taken from the Qur'ān. When the ceremony is over there is a festive meal for all the family and friends present.

Muslim boys are circumcised and this is also an occasion for family festivity. There is no hard and fast ruling about when **circumcision** should take place. Most Muslim parents arrange for it to be carried out at the local hospital if there are facilities available. No special religious ceremony is attached to the occasion but it is often celebrated with a family gathering and festive meal.

A   *Whispering the Iqamah in the baby's ear.*

Birth and naming

B   Muslims believe it is a privilege to bring up a child in the faith.

THINGS TO DO

1   With a partner work out your answers to the following questions:
   - What do you think is the meaning and purpose of whispering the call to prayer to the new-born child?
   - What do you think this ceremony means for the parents?
   - What does it tell us about a Muslim's beliefs about bringing up children?

2   The Prophet Muhammed said: 'Be careful of your duty to Allāh and be fair and just to your children.' What do you think he meant when he gave this advice to parents? What is the warning in this message? Discuss this in class and make up your own 'Sayings or warnings to parents'.

3   Design a card of congratulation at the birth of a child in a Muslim family. Remember that Muslims do not encourage the drawing or making of images of people or faces so as to avoid the risk of making idols. Choose a few words to put in your design.

4   In many religious communities a naming ceremony is important after the birth of a child. Design a naming ceremony for a non-religious family. Say who would be invited and what would take place and how it would be celebrated. Explain the meaning of your ceremony.

5   Imagine you are a Muslim and you have a new baby brother or sister. Describe the time they first hear the call to prayer, and the naming ceremony in your home as if you were writing to your grandmother who could not be there.

6   Names chosen for children are often significant in the family. Who chose your names and why? Make a class chart of the reasons behind your names being chosen.

Growing up in Islam

There is no special ceremony such as Baptism or Confirmation to celebrate the commitment of a believer in Islam. There is no initiation ceremony for entering the faith and no rite of passage which marks the beginning of adulthood for Muslims. Muslim children attend classes at the **mosque** from an early age so that they can read and speak the language of **Arabic** to recite the **Qur'ān**. Young Muslims learn about the faith and take on more responsibility for their own religion as they grow up but that does not make them any more Muslim than they were before.

Education is regarded as very important in Islam and young people are enouraged to devote much time to study. Learning Arabic and studying the Qur'ān is considered the most valuable education. Many Muslims would like their children to attend Muslim schools so that the teaching of the faith can play a more central role in their education.

Muslim girls are encouraged to dress modestly as they grow up and wear clothing that covers their arms and legs. For example, many Muslim girls whose families come from India or Pakistan wear a tunic and trousers called **kameez** and **shalwar** (B). This is to follow the teaching of the Qur'ān which says that dress should be modest. Muslim girls are generally not permitted to go out with boys and

A   *Learning the teachings of the Qur'ān is an important preparation for life.*

Growing up in Islam

Muslim schools have separate classes for girls and boys at secondary level. As Muslim boys approach adulthood they are expected to show greater respect towards the opposite sex.

The teachings of the Qur'ān mean more to young Muslims as they grow up and they become more aware of the difference between a life based on selfishness and a life which is based on the teachings of the Qur'ān. Sometimes it is difficult for a young person who has chosen a religious way of life to join in the activities in which their friends who are not religious are involved. This is when the young person most needs the support of his or her religious community. Many mosques in the UK now provide youth club activities for the young people in the Muslim community.

B Kameez and shalwar: dressing modestly does not need to be dull.

THINGS TO DO

1 Write down the things that make growing up in a religious tradition different from growing up in a family with no particular religious allegiance. Compare your list with that of a partner and share your ideas.

2 Muslims believe that there is no need for any special ceremony to express a person's commitment to Islam – it is enough to express it through one's daily life. Do you agree with this? Are special ceremonies important? In what way? Can they become meaningless? Discuss these questions in class.

3 Revise or look again at the main teachings of Islam. Use books from the bibliography on page 96 to help you. Write down the main guidelines on:
   - food
   - drink
   - dress
   - attitudes to parents and elders
   - behaviour towards the opposite sex.

4 Research shows that girls do better in their studies in single sex schools than in mixed schools. This could be a good case for keeping boys and girls separate. What other arguments could be brought to bear from a Muslim's point of view?

5 Look at Photo B. With a partner consider the differences you might find between these girls' daily life and your own. Write down the beliefs which account for these differences.

6 Most young people who are brought up in a faith keep to it. Others reject the family faith. Act out a scene where a young person is not sure about their parents' religion any more but the parents want them to keep to it. It can be in any religious tradition you choose.

34
Preparing for marriage

In the Islamic tradition parents believe that it is their duty as Muslims to seek out a suitable marriage partner for their son or daughter. They believe that people who have been married know best what to look for in a marriage partner. It is thought that such an important life-changing step should not depend on chance meetings. Young Muslims are discouraged from becoming too friendly with members of the opposite sex until they are ready to think about marriage.

Muslims prefer to call their approach 'assisted marriage' rather than 'arranged marriage'. This is because although the parents may be involved in introducing their child to a suitable person their child has the right to say no to the match. So the marriage is arranged after consultation with the young people involved. It cannot go ahead if one or both of the people involved opposes the arrangement.

In Islam marriage is seen as something which involves two families and not just two individuals. Since parents and sometimes grandparents are involved in choosing a suitable partner, they also carry some of the responsibility for the marriage being a success.

On the whole young Muslims trust their parents to find someone who will make a good husband or wife. Often the two families know each other and meetings are arranged between them so that the couple can get to see each other. If they are both interested then a meeting is arranged at the girl's home so that the couple can talk together. They are probably not marrying for love but may well be attracted to one another and find that they have things in common. An assisted marriage is not necessarily without romance. It is true, however, that love usually comes after marriage rather than before.

A   Muslims are encouraged to marry and have children.

Preparing for marriage

B *A Muslim family studying the Qur'ān together.*

The **Qur'ān** encourages Muslims to marry and have children. Happy family life is considered the basis of a happy society and so marriage is an important occasion in the Muslim community. Islamic law allows a man to have up to four wives. However, the husband must be fair to all his wives and show no favouritism. It is not surprising, therefore, that most Muslims have only one wife. Sexual relationships outside marriage are strictly forbidden according to Islamic law.

THINGS TO DO

1 Explain in your own words why Muslims prefer to speak of 'assisted marriage' rather than 'arranged marriage'.

2 Imagine you belong to a Muslim family. Your elder brother or sister is being introduced to a possible suitable marriage partner. The family has been invited to dinner. Write a sensitive and thoughtful diary entry on the subject and indicate your hopes for your brother or sister.

3 Discuss the good things about parents getting involved in finding a marriage partner for their son or daughter. Then discuss the difficulties that could arise. Suggest ways in which they could be overcome. Share your ideas in class.

4 'Happy family life is the basis of a happy society.' Is this true? What makes a happy family? Discuss this in small groups and then share your thoughts in class.

5 Sex outside marriage is not allowed according to Islamic law. This ruling is made for religious reasons. Draw up a list of other reasons why this is considered by many people to be a sensible ruling. Discuss your views on the matter with a friend.

6 What things do you think a Muslim parent will look for when seeking a suitable marriage partner for their son or daughter? Think carefully about their religious beliefs. What do you think they should consider? Discuss this in class.

A Muslim wedding

In Islam marriage is a human contract but Muslims believe that it is made before **Allāh**. Once the couple agree to marry the day for the wedding is set. The two families decide on a dowry called **mahr**. This is paid by the groom's family. Some of it is paid in goods which take the form of useful gifts for the married couple. The rest of the dowry is promised as security for the bride and remains her property.

In the UK the couple usually have a civil marriage before the Muslim wedding. The religious ceremony is often held at the bride's home or in a room or hall at the local mosque. Close friends and family are invited. The groom arrives at the bride's house with members of his family and guests.

The **imām** is invited to conduct the ceremony although this can be done by any Muslim man. The groom, his father and the other men present gather in a room where the imām begins by asking the groom if he consents to marry the bride. Once he has consented the groom then makes his marriage vows in the presence of the imām and witnesses. The bride does not have to be present for this. Her father can represent her. If she wishes she may wait in a separate room with the female members of the family where witnesses report to her when the groom has made his solemn promise:

'I — take — as my lawfully wedded wife before Allāh and in the presence of these witnesses, in accordance with the teachings of the holy Qur'ān.'

A   *In some communities the groom's face is veiled.*

A Muslim wedding

Allāh is called on as the supreme witness to this vow. The groom also promises to make the marriage an act of submission to Allāh, and a relationship of love, mercy and peace. The imām recites verses from the Qur'ān and prays for the welfare and happiness of the couple. Once the bride hears that the groom has made his promises she does the same, also in front of the imām and witnesses. The bride and groom then sign copies of the marriage contract and keep one each.

Sometimes the ceremony is followed by an old custom when the groom is presented with a glass of milk and traditional cakes to eat. These are from the bride and the women bring them to him. It is customary in some families for tricks to be played on the groom at this point. He must take the food and drink, no matter what they taste like, because they are a symbol of the hope for a family in the future. This is a social custom and not part of the religious ceremony.

Afterwards everybody is invited to celebrate with a festive meal. Then the bride and groom go to the groom's family home and live there until they are ready to set up home on their own.

THINGS TO DO

1   With a partner look through the Muslim wedding ceremony and write down the main differences between this and the sort of wedding you are familiar with. Discuss the possible reasons for these differences. What do they tell us about the different ideas on marriage?

2   Some parts of both wedding ceremonies are religious, some are social custom. Work out which is which and discuss your answers in class.

3   Imagine you are a close relative and witness at a Muslim wedding. Write an account of the proceedings in a letter to a relative who could not be present. Describe who was there and where the wedding took place. Say what part you played.

4   The Muslim wedding is a short and simple ceremony. So, too, is a civil wedding. What do you think are the essentials of a marriage ceremony?

5   Making vows or promises is an important part of most marriage ceremonies. What vows would you want your husband or wife to make? Write them down and discuss them with a partner. Do you think the vows should be the same for both men and women? Discuss these questions in class.

6   Many couples find their wedding a bit of a strain – all eyes are on them during what is an emotional occasion. Design a headdress or veil which could be worn at a wedding. Suggest reasons why it might be worn.

B   Muslim bride.

36

Life after death

Muslims believe that this life is a preparation for the life to come. In the teachings of the **Qur'ān** they learn that those who follow the will of **Allāh** find **paradise**. However, a Muslim should not serve Allāh just for the sake of future rewards. A **Sufi** poet wrote:

> O my Lord, if I worship Thee from fear of Hell, burn me in Hell, and if I worship Thee from hope of Paradise, exclude me thence, but if I worship Thee for Thine own sake then withhold not from me Thine Eternal Beauty.

A   *'Praise be to Allāh, Lord of the Creation . . .'*

The teachings of the holy Qur'ān promise a **Day of Resurrection**. Muslims believe that there will be a final judgement when everyone will be judged according to the life they have lead. The first chapter of the Qur'ān is a prayer for guidance to choose the path that leads to paradise in the life after death:

> In the name of Allāh, the Compassionate, the Merciful.
> Praise be to Allāh, Lord of the Creation,
> The Compassionate, the Merciful, King of Judgement Day
> You alone we worship and to You alone we pray for help
> Guide us to the straight path,
> The path of those whom You have favoured,
> Not of those who have incurred Your wrath
> Nor of those who have gone astray.

These words are recited in prayer each day. Evil must be overcome in this life through submission to the will of Allāh.

Life after death

The pilgrimage to **Makkah** is one of the **Five Pillars** of Islam. Every Muslim tries to join the **Hajj** at least once in their lifetime. Some older Muslims may see such a pilgrimage as a valuable way of preparing themselves for death. Many Mulims believe that performing Hajj can help to cleanse the soul of evil from all past actions.

Muslims believe that after the Resurrection those who have faithfully followed the path of Islam will be reunited with loved ones and enjoy all the blessings of paradise. Life after death is called **Ākhirah**. It is one of the basic beliefs of Islam. According to this belief wickedness and selfishness will be punished in the next life and goodness and faithfulness will be rewarded.

THINGS TO DO

1 With a partner write down some ideas you have between you about life after death. Discuss how they compare with the Muslim belief in a Day of Resurrection.

B   The Hajj: stoning the pillars at Mina is symbolic of fighting temptation.

2 Draw a chart, map or diagram (not using pictures of people) which gives an idea of the Muslim view of life and death and the life to come. Explain your illustration to a partner.

3 Write down some questions you might ask a Muslim on what they believe about life and death. With a partner write a short interview with a Muslim about their beliefs about evil, death and the Resurrection.

4 According to Islam, wickedness will not go unpunished. Do you think that belief in a Day of Judgement would influence the way you live your life? Discuss this with a partner. Share your ideas in class. Write up your own feelings on this matter.

5 The first chapter of the Qur'ān is used in prayer. Design a poster with these words using geometric design or plant and flower patterns. (Can you explain why only these should be used?)

6 Work in a group on a TV programme which considers beliefs about life after death. Make one of the people you interview a Muslim and explain carefully the Muslim point of view.

37

Muslim funeral rites

As a Muslim approaches death he or she will recite the words of the **Shahadah**. Close relatives or friends may read to them verses from the **Qur'ān**. When the person dies the family recite the following words from the Qur'ān:

> We belong to Allāh, and to him we shall return.

In Islam the body should be buried as soon as possible after death. Muslims believe that everyone will be raised from the dead. It is for this reason that the body is not destroyed by cremation but is shown great respect. The body is washed three times as if for prayer and then all over with soap and water. It is anointed with perfume and wrapped in three pieces of white cloth. In the UK the body is then laid in a coffin on its left side. The coffin is carried to the mosque and is placed so that the body faces **Makkah**. Prayers are said simply without the prayer movements and the first chapter of the Qur'ān is repeated. The coffin is taken to the cemetery for burial. As the coffin is lowered into the grave the following words from the Qur'ān are said:

> From the earth we did create you and into it we shall return and from it shall we bring you out once again.

These words remind Muslims of the **Day of Resurrection**.

Muslims believe that it is important for sons and daughters to pray for their parents after they have died, and to remember them and to visit their graves. When possible Muslims visit the graves of their dead relatives during **Eid ul Fitr**. This is the festival that ends the fast of **Ramadān**. Amid all the celebrations they remember that this life is temporary and that true joy will be found only in paradise.

A   Muslim funeral prayer.

Muslim funeral rites

B   Muslim burial.

In some parts of the world Muslims keep a special night called the **Night of Forgiveness** which falls on the eighth night of **Shab'an.** On this occasion Muslims believe that their life for the coming year is determined by Allāh. During the night Muslims spend time in prayer and many Muslims fast the day before. In some parts of the world Muslims visit the graves of loved ones to pay respect and to remember the Day of Resurrection (C).

1   Muslims pray for their loved ones who have died. What does this tell us of their beliefs about:
   ● God
   ● Allāh
   ● death
   ● the future of the dead?
   Work out your answers with a partner and discuss them in class.

2   The white cloths in which the body is dressed may have been worn before. When would this have been? What does this say about the meaning of the occasion for Muslims? Discuss this in class.

3   Revise what you have learned about Ramadān and Eid ul Fitr. Use the books in the bibliography on page 96 to find out more on these topics and write a couple of paragraphs explaining their significance for Muslims.

4   Imagine you belong to a Muslim household and an elderly relative has died. Describe the course of events from the death to the family visiting the grave. In your work try to explain what Muslims believe about life after death.

5   Many people find it difficult to imagine any life after death. With a partner write down all the difficulties and questions people might have concerning this belief. Discuss them in class. Set up a class debate on the question of life after death.

6   Muslims believe that there will be a time when they will meet their loved ones again after death. This is one of the promises of paradise. What is your idea of 'paradise'? What would you look for in paradise after death? Discuss your ideas with a partner and then write a poem or piece of prose called 'In Paradise'.

C   Muslims visiting the graves of the dead.

Sikhism: many lives, one journey

Sikhs believe that this human existence is not the first time we have lived on earth. They believe that the soul lives through numerous existences and is reborn or reincarnated in different forms. After many births the soul eventually reaches the human level of existence. It is only at this stage in the soul's journey that it can attain **mukti**. Mukti means liberation from the endless cycle of reincarnation.

Sikhs believe that there is one God. Sometimes he is called **Sat Nam**, the True Name, or **Waheguru**, Wonderful Lord. It is God who awakens the human soul and calls men and women to him. Sikhs believe that it is God's will that all people should come to know and worship him so that he can abide in them and by his grace they can attain liberation.

The teachings of the Sikh holy scriptures, the **Guru Granth Sahib**, show that the way to liberation can be found in everyday life. That is, the sort of life in which every action is made an act of devotion to God. Every thought and deed then becomes a prayer and the believer draws closer and closer to union with God. It is through union with God that the soul becomes free.

B   Sikhs at worship.

A person only survives and grows physically if they belong to a caring community which feeds and protects its members. A person only develops towards spiritual and moral perfection if they belong to a community which nurtures them spiritually and morally. The Sikh faith provides an example of the sort of community in which all aspects of human development are cared for. This community is called the **Sangat**. The Sangat is an ideal society in miniature where humility, tolerance, patience, service, justice, mercy and kindness are encouraged and acted out in practical ways. These qualities are an expression of knowledge and love of God.

A   The Guru Granth Sahib.

The **Gurdwara** is the place where the Sikh Sangat is able to serve the wider community. The **langar** provides food for physical nourishment (C). Worship at the Gurdwara provides spiritual nourishment through the reading of the scriptures, prayer and devotional hymns or **kirtan**.

Sikhism: many lives, one journey

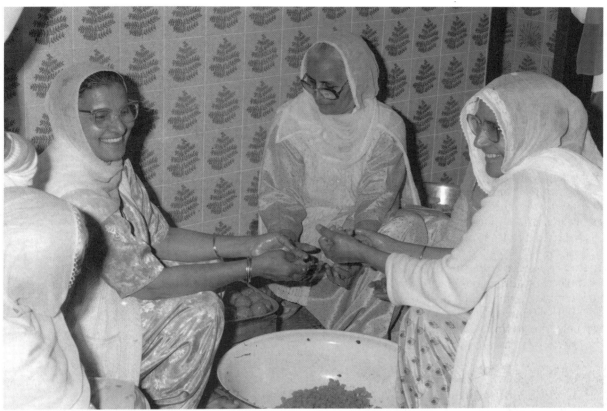

C   *Preparing food at the langar.*

THINGS TO DO

1   Draw a diagram, map or chart which explain the Sikh view of human existence as a path towards liberation. Try to show how human birth is not the beginning of the soul's existence and how the soul lives many lives. Compare the Sikh view of human existence with the other lifemaps you have been looking at.

2   Revise or look again at the life and work of the Sikh community at the Gurdwara. Use the books mentioned in the bibliography on page 96 to help you. Make up a wordsearch using some of the vocabulary you have learned from the Sikh tradition.

3   Many people feel that this life is not the only one they have lived. What arguments and ideas might be used to support this view? Discuss this in class.

4   Do you think that our society and culture encourage moral and spiritual development? What things would help people to develop in this way? Discuss this in class and then write a summary of your ideas.

5   With a partner make a list of the qualities you think we should develop in life. How does your list compare with the qualities to be encouraged according to Sikhism?

6   'No man is an island.' Is this true? To what extent do you think we can live without others? To what extent do we depend on others to survive? Discuss your ideas in class.

39

The Sikh naming ceremony

According to Sikhism this human life is a precious gift. It is an opportunity to know God and to find union with him. Birth is therefore a time for rejoicing and giving thanks to God.

In a Sikh family, a few days after the birth of a child, the parents take the baby to the **Gurdwara** for the naming ceremony (A). Usually, friends and relatives are invited too. As people enter they make offerings of money or food and bow before the **Guru Granth Sahib**.

The child's name is then chosen. The granthi takes the Guru Granth Sahib and lets the pages fall open at random. He then turns to the first word of the first hymn on the left-hand page. Whatever letter this word begins with decides the first letter of the child's name. Once the parents have chosen the first name they tell the granthi the child's name, the granthi announces it and says a blessing. Prayers are recited and a special prayer for the child included which

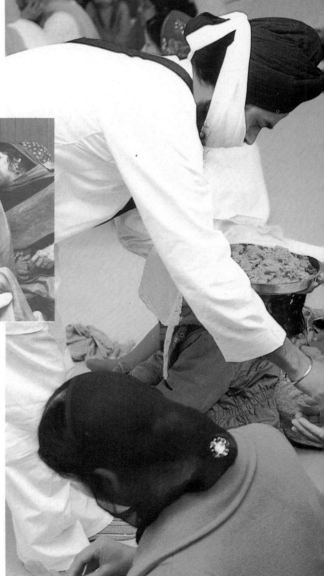

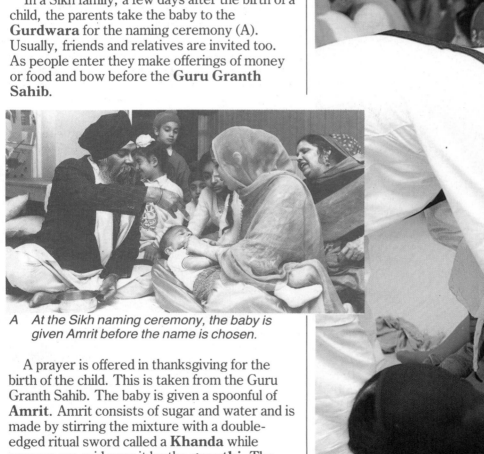

A At the Sikh naming ceremony, the baby is given Amrit before the name is chosen.

A prayer is offered in thanksgiving for the birth of the child. This is taken from the Guru Granth Sahib. The baby is given a spoonful of **Amrit**. Amrit consists of sugar and water and is made by stirring the mixture with a double-edged ritual sword called a **Khanda** while prayers are said over it by the **granthi**. The granthi is the person who leads the worship in the readings from the Guru Granth Sahib at the Gurdwara. At the naming ceremony, the granthi dips the sword in the Amrit and very lightly touches the baby's tongue and head with the tip of the sword. The rest of the ritual mixture is given to the mother to drink.

expresses the hope that they will become a true Sikh and show devotion to God. After the ceremony **karah parshad** is shared out among those present. This is blessed food and is a symbol of God's goodness and blessings to all humankind. The sharing of food is also a sign of equality and of belonging to one great 'family'. Sometimes the family choose to give a special gift to the Gurdwara to show their thankfulness and to mark the birth of their child.

The Sikh naming ceremony

THINGS TO DO

1 Giving, gifts and blessings are important themes at the naming ceremony. With a partner find all the references to giving and gifts. Discuss them and write down the meaning behind them.

2 Some parents arrange to have an **Akhand Path** to celebrate the birth of a child in the family. This is a continuous and uninterrupted reading of the Guru Granth Sahib. On what other occasions does this reading take place? Find out from the books in the bibliography on page 96 and from what you have learned previously.

3 Write a newspaper article for your local paper explaining what happens at the Sikh naming ceremony. You could write up an imaginary interview with the Sikh parents of a new baby who tell you what the ceremony means for them.

4 According to many religious people life is an opportunity to grow in knowledge of God. What opportunities do you see in life? Discuss this question in class.

5 All Sikh names mean something. For example, Gurbakhsh Singh means 'Blessed by the Guru'. It is hoped that the life or character of the child will be shaped by a good name. What names do you know that indicate a certain quality of character?

6 Imagine you belong to a Sikh family. Your baby brother or sister is being taken to the Gurdwara for the naming ceremony. Imagine you have questions to ask your mother or father about the meaning of the ceremony. Write up the conversation with your parents as a sort of play.

B Sharing out the karah parshad: purity, generosity and community life are important in the Sikh tradition.

Life as a spiritual journey

Guru Nanak, the first of the **Ten Gurus** (A), denounced the divisions which had developed between people in India in his time. He refused to acknowledge the split between Hindu and Muslim and called men and women to worship God as one. He rejected the barriers of class and **caste** which divided people and led to fear and injustice. Guru Nanak and his followers also refused to believe that there were obstacles preventing people from gaining liberation. He taught that traditional beliefs about separate stages in life restricted spiritual growth.

Sikhs believe that everyone should be a spiritual seeker at every stage in life and not wait until they reach the end of their lives. The whole of life is a spiritual journey in which God is the goal. Sikhs believe that the way to liberation is open to everyone, no matter what their background, their religion or the stage they are at in life.

Sikhism also rejects what it sees as the meaningless and hypocritical ceremonies and rituals of religion. Instead of concentrating on ceremony Sikhism aims to encourage moral values and spiritual development. For this purpose the **Gurdwara** is open for people to listen to the teachings of the **Guru Granth Sahib.** The ceremonies which Sikhs do practise are intended to remind believers of the importance of devotion to God and of their moral responsibilities.

One important Sikh ceremony is called Amrit taking, or **Amrit-pan karna.** It was introduced by **Guru Gobind Singh** (B) when Sikhs were facing bitter persecution. He saw that to survive, Sikhs would have to be ready to fight for justice and freedom and be willing to risk their lives in the face of persecution. Guru Gobind Singh found five such men. They showed such dedication and courage that they were willing to die for the faith. Guru Gobind Singh initiated these five believers with **Amrit.**

A   The Gurus, including Guru Nanak

Life as a spiritual journey

This was a mixture made with sugar and water and blessed with readings from the scriptures. The five became known as the **Panj Piare** (Five Pure Ones). They took a vow to follow the teachings of the Ten Gurus and were the first members of the **Khalsa**. This is the body of Sikhs who have taken Amrit and have dedicated themselves to the service of God.

B Guru Gobind Singh, who introduced the Amrit ceremony and began the Khalsa.

THINGS TO DO

1   With a partner make a list of the barriers dividing people in our society today. In what ways can such barriers be overcome? Discuss your answers in class.

2   Sikhs believe that anyone can gain salvation and there is no need to opt out of everyday life in search of truth. Do you think this is reasonable or do you think that a person needs to give up the things of this world in order to find the truth? Discuss this in class.

3   In what practical ways does Sikhism try to break down barriers? Design a poster which shows how the Sikh faith aims to break down barriers between people and open the way to liberation.

4   Look again at the story of Guru Gobind Singh and the beginning of the Khalsa. Write a checklist of points to remember about the event. Use the books in the bibliography on page 96 to help you.

5   Invite a Sikh to speak to the class about the way in which Sikhs try to find union with God in their everyday lives. Prepare a set of questions to ask your visitor.

6   Sikhism grew up in India where most people are Hindus. Sikhs and Hindus have certain beliefs in common. Try to work out some of the beliefs they share and also the major differences between them.

Amrit-pan karna

Today Amrit taking marks the time when a Sikh makes a full commitment to the faith and becomes a member of the Sikh **Khalsa**. Sikh men and women can come forward for this ceremony at any age. Some Sikhs receive Amrit a second time if they have lapsed from the faith and want to renew their commitment later in life. Most Sikhs who choose to take Amrit do so as they approach adulthood and are old enough to understand the responsibilities and commitments they are taking on.

A   *Young Sikhs at their Amrit ceremony.*

The ceremony today is held at the **Gurdwara**. The Sikhs receiving Amrit prepare for the ceremony. They bathe, wash their hair and put on clean clothes. Five members of the Khalsa, called the **Panj Piare** and wearing the **Five Ks** (B), perform the ceremony. The novices stand before them and promise to dedicate their lives to the teachings of the faith. The Panj Piare pray for God's help and blessing in the ceremony. The **granthi** then reads a passage from the pages of the **Guru Granth Sahib**. The Panj Piare prepare a bowl of Amrit. Each of them takes the bowl in turn and stirs the mixture with the double-edged sword. Many prayers are recited over the Amrit, including the **Japji** from the words of **Guru Nanak**. The bowl is raised up for all to see and God's blessing is asked on those receiving Amrit.

Amrit-pan karna

They are to pray daily, every morning before dawn and after sunset and before going to bed

They are to wear the Five Ks and not cut their hair

They must refrain from intoxicating drink and cigarettes

They are to be faithful in marriage.

After this ceremony the boys receive the name **Singh**, meaning lion and the girls receive the name **Kaur**, meaning princess. Traditionally these names replaced the family name, to break down barriers between people caused by differences in background. The **Ardas**, the prayer that comes at the close of Sikh worship, is recited and everyone receives **karah parshad** at the end of the service.

THINGS TO DO

1   Taking Amrit is a serious occasion for a young Sikh. What are the most serious occasions in the life of a young person? Discuss this question in class. Describe such an occasion in writing.

2   Do people make promises too easily? Discuss this with a partner. Draw up a list of occasions when people make serious promises. What are the most important promises a person makes in their life?

3   Imagine you have recently become a member of the Khalsa. Write a letter to a friend telling them about the ceremony and your promises and hopes to become a true Sikh.

4   Design a greetings card which could be sent to a Sikh about to receive Amrit and enter the Khalsa. Use the Five Ks as symbols in your design.

5   Imagine you are a parent, happy to see your son or daughter receive Amrit. Write a diary page expressing your feelings and hopes for the child.

6   Some people call Amrit-pan karna the Sikh baptism. Does it have anything in common with the Christian ceremonies of Infant or Believer's Baptism? Discuss the differences and similarities with a partner and decide whether baptism is a good translation for the Amrit ceremony.

B   Sikhs wearing the Five Ks.

Each of the novices comes forward in turn and kneels before the Panj Piare. The Amrit is given five times into their cupped hands to drink. It is sprinkled five times over their eyes and five times on their heads. This symbolizes the intention to refrain from evil and to grow in the faith. Then they declare: 'The Khalsa is dedicated to God. The victory belongs to God alone'. All those who have received Amrit drink the remaining nectar from the same bowl. Finally, they recite the **Mool Mantra** five times declaring belief in one God. The Panj Piare remind them of their vows to live according to the teachings of the **Ten Gurus**:

Sikh marriage

Sikhs believe that marriage is the union of two people in body, mind and soul. They believe that it enables two people to grow spiritually and morally through a close relationship built on respect, love and faithfulness. In Sikhism marriage is for life. The choice of partner is therefore very important. Sikh parents consider it their duty to find a suitable marriage partner for their son or daughter. However, the young person is involved in the decision and does not have to accept their parents' choice. In the case of disagreement the proposal is dropped and the search for another partner begins. It is usual among Sikhs to have a betrothal ceremony once a decision has been made. This takes place at the girl's home.

Before the religious marriage ceremony most Sikhs will have a **register office** wedding as not all Gurdwaras have been officially registered for weddings in the UK. The Sikh wedding is called **Anand Karaj** which means the 'Ceremony of Bliss'. It is held early in the morning and must take place in the presence of the **Guru Granth Sahib**. It is often held at the Gurdwara. The service begins with the musicians singing hymns. The bride and groom sit facing the Holy Scriptures. The person conducting the service reminds the couple of the seriousness of the occasion, the responsibilities they have towards one another and the importance of faithfulness, kindness and humility in marriage.

The couple are asked if it is their wish to be married. This ensures that neither is being married against their will. They show their acceptance by bowing before the Guru Granth Sahib. The bride's father then takes the scarf worn by the groom and puts one end into the groom's right hand and the other end into the hand of his daughter. Then the musicians sing a celebration hymn before the reading of the Guru Granth Sahib. The **granthi** reads a special hymn called the **Lavan** from the scriptures. This hymn reminds the couple of

A *'They are not man and wife who only have physical contact; only they are wedded truly who have one spirit in two bodies'. These words of Guru Amar Das, one of the Ten Gurus, are often recited at wedding ceremonies.*

their religious commitments. With each verse sung by the musicians, the bride and groom, linked together, walk in a complete circle around the Guru Granth Sahib (B). The words of the last verse of the Lavan compare the union between husband and wife to the union between God and the human soul. In this way it is said that marriage can bring spiritual insight and growth. At the end of the fourth verse the couple complete their fourth circle and are declared man and wife. They are then showered with flower petals. The granthi comes forward and congratulates the couple and the congregation stand for the closing prayer. The last word is from the Guru Granth Sahib when the granthi again opens the pages of the holy book, this time at random, and reads a verse to close the ceremony before the **karah parshad** is offered to everyone.

Usually the ceremony is followed by a festive meal and family celebration. The bride then joins the groom at his home and begins her life as a part of his family.

Sikh marriage

1   Do you think that marriage can help an individual grow into a better person? In what ways? Discuss this with a partner. Make a list of important points and then share ideas in class.

2   There are some important symbolic actions and symbols at work in the marriage ceremony. What are they and what do they mean? Write your answers first and then discuss them in class.

3   Design a Sikh wedding invitation which shows the importance of the Guru Granth Sahib in the ceremony.

4   The bride usually has a friend who provides help and support before the wedding and assists throughout the ceremony. Imagine you are such a helper or a relative. Describe what happens at the wedding and how you felt about the ceremony. Use Photos A and B to help you.

5   The union between husband and wife is compared to the union between God and the soul. What do you think is meant by this comparison? Can you think of ways in which it helps people understand their relationship with God? Discuss this in class.

6   Marriage and family life are believed to be desirable in Sikhism. They bring blessings and benefits both to the couple and to society. In what ways do you think married life is a desirable kind of life? Is it selfish not to marry? Discuss these questions in pairs and then open up the discussion to the class as a whole.

B   *Sikh bride and groom circling the Guru Granth Sahib.*

43

Death and cremation

Sikhs believe that it is possible to find liberation in this life by the grace of God. However, if the soul does not attain liberation it will be born again in another body and continue its journey towards union with God and release from earthly existence. The soul cannot go backwards. Once it has reached the human sphere it can only move on towards liberation although it may take many births.

At death the soul is released either to be united with God or to return to the cycle of **reincarnation**. When someone dies the family joins in the words of prayers and hymns from the **Guru Granth Sahib**. It is in the words of the scriptures that the family finds comfort and courage at this time.

Close members of the family are responsible for the arrangements for the funeral and the services of an undertaker are usually employed.

The body is washed with a mixture made from water and yoghurt which has purifying qualities. The body is dressed in clean clothes and if the person was a male member of the **Khalsa** the body is dressed in the Four Ks, with the hair uncut being the fifth K. The turban is placed on the head if the dead person is male. Sikhs cremate their dead. In the UK the cremation takes place at the crematorium (B).

On the day of the cremation prayers are said for the soul of the dead person and the coffin is taken in a hearse to the crematorium. Close family members are present at this simple ceremony when prayers are said over the coffin before it is taken away for cremation. Friends and relatives go to the crematorium and usually there is a service afterwards at the **Gurdwara** where everyone gathers. After a few days the ashes are collected from the crematorium and thrown into the flowing waters of a nearby river.

At the Gurdwara the granthi recites readings from the Guru Granth Sahib. There are many words of hope and comfort in the hymns of the **Ten Gurus**. There is hymn called **Kirtan Sohila** – the Evening Prayer – which is quite often sung at a funeral:

> Know the real purpose of being here and gather up your treasure under the guidance of the true Guru. Make your mind God's home. If he abides with you undisturbed, you will not be reborn.

Sometimes people will want to say a few words about the person who has died to show respect and love. The service ends as usual with the **Ardas** and sweet karah parshad is shared out amongst all present. Some Sikhs like to follow the funeral with an **Akhand Path** which is an uninterrupted reading of the Guru Granth Sahib in the home. However, the usual practice is to commission a reading of the Guru Granth Sahib at the Gurdwara or in the home of the deceased person, to be completed in about ten days when there will be a final gathering of friends and relatives, an opportunity for people to give their condolences for the last time.

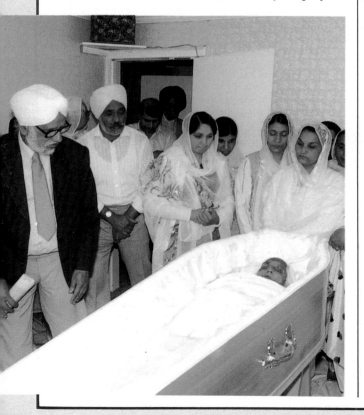

A   Sikh coffin and mourners.

Death and cremation

B *Sikhs may have to use a Christian chapel at the crematorium.*

THINGS TO DO

1 Compare the Sikh beliefs about death with the beliefs of other religions. Discuss some of the differences and similarities between the Sikh, Hindu and Buddhist views.

2 'Know the real purpose of being here.' Write down some of your own ideas on the 'purpose of being here'. With a partner compare your ideas with the Sikh teachings on life and its purpose.

3 Imagine you are a member of the Sikh community and someone in the community has recently died who had been a well loved member of the Khalsa. Write a short account of the cremation and ceremony at the Gurdwara for the community newspaper.

4 Write a poem or 'Evening Prayer' which could be said at a service for the death of a friend or loved one.

5 Chapels at most crematoriums have the Christian symbol of a cross. Some people feel that crematorium chapels should not be exactly like a Christian chapel as people of different beliefs use them. Set up a class debate with speakers on one side arguing for the chapel remaining Christian and speakers on the other arguing against.

6 Arrange a class visit to a Gurdwara to find out about the ceremonies associated with birth, marriage and death in the Sikh religion. Prepare a set of questions to ask members of the community when you are there. Write up a class project on these ceremonies and their meaning.

44
Further study

Use books from the bibliography on page 96 to help you with these activities.

1 Look at the two invitations to special occasions. Describe what happens at each of these ceremonies. Say what the occasion means to the believers present at the ceremony in each case. Give some of your own thoughts on the importance and value of these occasions. Draw out points of similarity and important points of difference between the two ceremonies and their meaning for the communities involved.

Mr and Mrs Goldstein
of

104 Keighton Hill
Manley Heath
Winton

*invite you to the
Brit Milah of their son*

Brit Milah
at the Orthodox Synagogue
Manley Heath
at 12 noon, 25 October
and after, at home

R.S.V.P

*Mr and Mrs Smith
invite you to celebrate the birth of their daughter
Mary*

*and to join them at her Baptism
at: the Parish Church of All Saints, Henstead
at: 11 AM, Sunday 14 May*

*and after at:
24 High Street, Henstead*

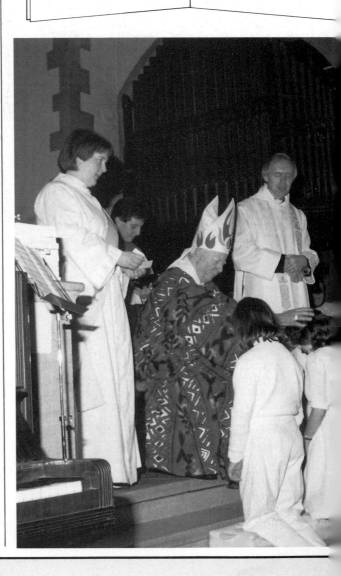

2 Look at the photos. Imagine you are present at each of these occasions. Write an article for a church magazine describing the occasions and the meaning of the ceremony for the believers in each church. Include an interview with someone who was taking part in the ceremony in each case. At the end of the article write about the important differences between the two ceremonies and the beliefs involved. Say what you think are the most important differences and explain why.

3 Prepare a project on marriage and wedding ceremonies using examples from at least two religions. Illustrate your work showing the symbols involved where relevant. Explain the meaning of the ceremonies for the people involved. Suggest reasons why so many couples/families choose a religious ceremony to celebrate marriage. Say what you consider to be the most important aspects of a wedding ceremony and explain why.

4 Prepare a series of interviews for a TV religious programme. Choose representatives from three religions to be interviewed. Write up questions on the following:
- Beliefs about death and the question of life after death.
- Funeral customs and the meaning of these rituals for the communities involved.

In a group work out the answers believers from the different faiths might give.

Glossary

A

Adhān Muslim call to prayer

Agni Hindu god of fire

Akhand Path complete and uninterrupted reading of the **Guru Granth Sahib**

Ākhira Arabic word for 'Life after Death'

Allāh Arabic word for God

Alms charity, gift of food

Altar table in a church representing the table of the **Last Supper**

Amrit blessed and sweetened water used in Sikh ceremonies; the Sikh initiation ceremony

Amrit-pan karna Sikh ceremony for those joining the **Khalsa**

Anand Karaj Sikh wedding ceremony

Anglican belonging to the Church of England

Aqiqah Muslim ceremony giving thanks for the birth of a child in which a sacrifice is made

Arabic the language of the Holy **Qur'ān**

Ardas Sikh prayer said at the **Gurdwara** service

Ark cupboard in a **synagogue** to hold the sacred scrolls of the **Torah**

Arranged marriage traditional marriage in which the family is involved in finding a suitable marriage partner for the son or daughter

Arti offering of light in Hindu worship

Ashrama stage in life in Hindu tradition for **Brahmins**, **Kshatriyas** and **Vaishyas**

Assisted marriage a marriage in which the family will take care to introduce the son or daughter to suitable marriage partners but the final decision remains with the couple

Atman Hindu word for an individual soul

B

Baptism ceremony to represent the start of a new life, sometimes involving total immersion, sometimes sprinkling with water

Baptistry pool for baptism

Bar Mitzvah 'Son of the Commandment'; Jewish boys become Bar Mitzvah at the age of 13; a ceremony to mark a boy's Bar Mitzvah

Bat Mitzvah 'Daughter of the Commandment'; ceremony to mark a girl's coming of age in the Jewish religion

Believer's Baptism ceremony of total immersion in water in Baptist Church to mark personal commitment to Christ and the beginning of a new life

Bhajan Hindu hymn of praise

Bhikkhu Buddhist monk

Bhikkhuni Buddhist nun

Bible the Christian Holy Scriptures

Bimah reading desk in the **synagogue** from where the **Torah** is read

Bishop senior figure of authority in **Anglican**, **Orthodox** and **Roman Catholic** traditions, usually attached to a cathedral

Bodhisatta Buddhist saintly being who helps people to enlightenment

Brahma charya the student stage in life according to Hindu tradition

Brahman Hindu term meaning 'Supreme Spirit of the Universe'; God

Brahmin Hindu priest; someone belonging to the priestly caste

Breaking of Bread Christian service with bread and wine or grape juice commemorating the **Last Supper**

Brit Milah 'Covenant of Cutting', Jewish rite of **circumcision**

Buddha Buddhist term meaning 'Enlightened One'; Gotama Buddha

C

Caste division in Hindu society according to family or occupation

Catholic *see* **Roman Catholic**

Christ 'Anointed One' or 'King' (in Hebrew 'Messiah'); title given to Jesus

Christening Infant Baptism in the **Anglican**, **Orthodox** and **Roman Catholic** traditions

Chuppah canopy representing the harmony of the home in a Jewish wedding

Church community of followers of Christ; body of Christians; building for Christian worship

Circumcision the cutting and removal of the foreskin; rite practised in the Jewish and Muslim traditions

Communion *see* **Holy Communion** and **Eucharist**

Confession thoughts, words or prayers asking God's forgiveness in the Christian tradition

Confirmation a Christian sacrament in which the believer makes firm their commitment in the faith

Consecrate to make sacred with a blessing or ritual performed by a priest in the Christian tradition

Covenant sacred agreement made between God and his people in the Jewish tradition

Cremation the burning of a corpse to reduce it to ashes

Crematorium place where there is a furnace and chapel for carrying out cremations and funeral services

D

Day of Resurrection Moslim belief in a final day of judgement when **Allāh** will raise the dead to life

Dedication church service in which Christian parents bring their baby to be blessed and give thanks to God

Deity god or image of a god

Dhamma teachings of the Buddha

Dharma Hindu word for religion meaning 'Law' or 'What is right' or simply 'Duty'

Diwan Sikh congregational worship

Dukkha Buddhist term meaning 'suffering' or 'unsatisfactoriness'

E

Elijah early Hebrew prophet; herald of the **Messianic Age** in Jewish tradition

Enlightenment liberation from the bonds of earthly life; translation of terms **Nibbana** and **moksha**

Eid ul Adha Muslim festival of sacrifice

Eid ul Fitr Muslim festival of fast breaking after **Ramadān**

Eucharist 'thanksgiving'; Christian service where bread and wine are shared, also known as **Mass**, **Holy Communion**, and the **Lord's Supper**

F

Fast to go without food or certain types of food and drink as a religious duty

Father, Son and Holy Spirit the three aspects of the Christian Godhead; the Trinity

Five Ks five religious symbols worn by Sikhs: Kesh – uncut hair, Kara – steel bracelet, Kangha – comb, Kach – shorts, and Kirpan – symbolic sword

Five Pillars of Islam basis of Muslim faith

Font container for water in a church used for **Infant Baptism**

Four Noble Truths the first teachings of the Buddha

G

Gayatri Mantra Hindu daily prayer asking for **enlightenment**

Genesis the first book of the **Torah**, also the first book of the **Bible**

Godparents people chosen by Christian parents to take a special interest in the religious upbringing of their child and who represent the child at **Infant Baptism**

Granthi the leader in Sikh worship at the Gurdwara who reads from the **Guru Granth Sahib**

Grihastha householder stage in life in Hindu tradition

Gurdwara Sikh place of worship where the **Guru Granth Sahib** is installed

Guru religious or spiritual teacher in the Hindu tradition

Guru Granth Sahib the Sikh holy book

Guru Nanak the first of the Sikh founders

Guru Gobind Singh one of the Sikh founders who established the **Khalsa**

H

Hajj fifth pillar of Islam, the pilgrimage to **Makkah**

Halāl permitted meat prepared according to Islamic law

Havan Hindu fire ritual

Heaven the belief in existence after death in which the souls of the faithful are rewarded; a blissful existence in the eternal presence of God

Hebrew the language of the Jewish people; the language of the Jewish scriptures

Hell the belief in an existence after death in which the souls of the wicked are punished

Holy Communion Christian service in which bread and wine are shared in remembrance of the **Last Supper**

Holy Spirit the power and presence of God on earth in Christian tradition, sometimes called the Holy Ghost

Host the bread or wafer representing the body of Christ in the service of **Mass**

I

Imām leader of prayer in Muslim public worship

Infant Baptism Christian rite in which a baby is anointed with consecrated water and welcomed into the Church in **Anglican, Orthodox** and **Roman Catholic** traditions

Initiation ritual or ceremony in which a person is officially made a member of a religious community

Iqamah words of prayer whispered into the ear of a baby in the Muslim tradition

Israel the worldwide community of Jews; the land of Israel or the modern state of Israel

J

Japji words of **Guru Nanak**; hymn used in Sikh daily prayer

K

Kaaba the most sacred building for Muslims dedicated to Allāh

Kaddish Jewish prayer of blessing said in funeral or mourning ceremonies at the **synagogue**

Kadosh 'holy' in Hebrew

Kameez tunic top worn by many Muslim girls whose family background is Pakistan or the Indian subcontinent

Karah parshad blessed sweet pudding shared out at end of Sikh service at the Gurdwara

Karma 'actions'; the law of cause and effect according to Hindu tradition

Kaur 'Princess', name given to Sikh girls at the **Amrit ceremony**

Ketubah Jewish marriage contract

Khalsa the community of 'the Pure Ones'; the body of committed Sikhs

Khanda double-edged ritual sword used in Sikh **Amrit ceremony**

Kiddushin Hebrew word for the wedding ceremony in Judaism

Kirtan Sikh devotional hymn

Kirtan Sohila devotional hymn sung at Sikh funeral service

Kosher food that is 'fit' according to Jewish law

Kshatriya warrior or princely class in Hindu traditional society

L

Langar kitchen at the Sikh Gurdwara; community meal after Sikh service

Last Supper Jesus' last meal with his disciples before his death

Lavan hymn from **Guru Granth Sahib** sung at Sikh wedding

Lay community ordinary men and women of a religious community who are not monks, nuns or priests

Lord's Supper *see* **Eucharist**

Liberal with reference to Jewish community – those who interpret the **Torah** with greater freedom than the **Orthodox** community

M

Mahr dowry in Muslim marriage which remains property of wife

Mahayana 'The Great Way'; one of the two main branches of Buddhism

Makkah Mecca, the city where Muhammad was born

Mandir Hindu temple

Mantra sacred hymn or chant in Hindu and Sikh traditions

Mass *see* **Eucharist**

Meditation a process of disciplining the mind to attain control of the body, mind and senses or to gain spiritual insight; prayerful reflection

Glossary

Messiah Hebrew word meaning 'Anointed One' or 'King'

Messianic Age New age of peace in Jewish tradition in which God's representative or God's people will establish God's reign on earth

Minister a leader of a church or a preacher in the non-conformist churches; a general term for vicar or priest

Mohel a trained person who performs the Jewish rite of circumcision

Moksha Hindu word for 'Liberation' or 'Salvation'; release from the cycle of **karma** and **samsara**

Mool Mantra **Guru Nanak's** words on God used in Sikh prayer

Mosque 'place of prostration'; Muslim place of prayer

Muhammad Allāh's messenger, the last and most important prophet according to Islam

Mukti Sikh term for 'Liberation' from eternal cycle of reincarnation; a state of bliss in the presence of God

N

Nam Sikh word for the holy Name of God

New Testament second part of the Christian **Bible**

Nibbana 'blown out', Buddhist word for liberation from the bonds of earthly life; enlightenment

Night of Forgiveness a special night of prayer and fasting when Muslims remember the Day of Judgement

O

Om Hindu sacred sound and symbol used in meditation and worship meaning the eternal truth

Old Testament the first part of the Christian **Bible**

Ordination ceremony at which a person is accepted into an order of monks or nuns; ceremony for initiation into a priesthood

Orthodox with reference to Judaism – those who maintain a traditional interpretation of the **Torah** and who reject the interpretations of the Liberal and Reform Jews

Orthodox those branches of the Christian Church which are traditionally found in Russia, Greece and Eastern Europe

P

Pali traditional language of the **Theravadin** Buddhist scriptures

Panj Piare the 'Five Pure Ones' also known as the 'Five Beloved Ones' in the Sikh tradition

Paradise a place or state of harmony and happiness promised after death

Pbuh 'Peace be upon him'; Muslims put this after the name of Muhammad as a sign of respect

Pesach Jewish festival commemorating the Exodus of Moses and the people of Israel out of Egypt

Prashad Sikh blessed food

Priest religious leader; in Anglican, Orthodox and Roman Catholic traditions priests are ordained through which it is believed they receive the authority given by Christ to Peter

Prophet someone sent by God to speak his message

Protestant those churches which do not accept the authority of the Pope and do not belong to the Orthodox community of Christians

Puja offerings and acts of devotion at a Buddhist shrine

Q

Qur'ān the sacred scriptures of Muslims

R

Rabbi teacher; religious leader in the Jewish community

Rama an incarnation of the Hindu God **Vishnu**

Ramadān the Muslim month of fasting

Rebirth being born into a new life

Reform in the Jewish context, the community of Jews who have adapted their worship and practice to respond to modern-day living

Register Office a local office set up for the registration of marriages for official purposes

Resurrection belief in the continuity of life after death; Christian belief in Christ risen from the dead

Revelation something that has been revealed to humankind; sacred scripture or given truth

Rite of passage a ceremony or ritual marking the major turning points in the human life cycle

Roman Catholic the Christian community that accepts the authority of the Pope as head of the Church

S

Sacrament an outward sign or symbolic action carrying spiritual blessing or power

Sacrifice an offering that is of personal cost

Salvation Army a Christian evangelical church founded by William Booth

Salah Muslim set prayer; one of the Five Pillars of Islam

Samsara Hindu belief in the eternal cycle of reincarnation

Sandek male relative or friend who holds the baby at the Jewish rite of **Brit Milah**

Sangha community of Buddhist monks and nuns

Sangat Sikh congregation of worshippers

Sanskrit traditional language of the Hindu scriptures, the **Vedas**, an ancient language of India

Sannyasin someone who has given up worldly attachments to seek spiritual truth; final stage in life in Hindu tradition

Sat Nam 'The True Name', Sikh name for God

Saum Muslim fast, one of the Five Pillars of Islam

Shab'an a month on the Islamic calendar

Shabbat Jewish day of rest

Shahadah Muslim declaration of faith

Shalwar leggings or trousers worn by many Muslim girls whose family background is Pakistan or the Indian subcontinent

Shema verses from the **Torah** containing the core beliefs of the Jewish faith

Shiva Hindu god, Lord of Destruction

Sigálvada Sutta Buddhist scripture concerned with the life of the lay community

Sin evil or wrongdoing; separation from God; disobedience

Singh 'Lion', name given to Sikh boys and men at the **Amrit ceremony**

Sita wife of the Hindu god Rama

Soul a personal spirit or self which is not body

Sufi Muslim from the mystic tradition

Sukkoth   Jewish autumn Feast of Tabernacles
Synagogue   'Gathering Place', Jewish place of worship

T

Takht   platform in **Gurdwara** from where the scriptures are read
Tallit   Jewish prayer shawl
Talmud   the body of interpretation and discussion on the **Torah**
Ten Gurus   the founders of the Sikh faith
Tenakh   the **Torah**, Nevi'im and Ketuvi'im which make up the Jewish scriptures (The Law, The Prophets and The Writings)
Tephilin   scrolls in tiny leather boxes containing the words of the **Shema** from the **Torah**
Theravada   the 'Way of the Elders', the older of the two main branches of Buddhism
Torah   the Five Books of Moses, sometimes called the Law, the most important of the Jewish scriptures

U

Upanayam   the Hindu Sacred Thread ceremony

V

Vanaprastha   the third stage in life according to Hindu tradition

Glossary

Vaishyas   the merchant class in traditional Hindu society
Varna   traditional class division in Hindu society
Vedas   the most ancient and most important of the Hindu scriptures
Vicar   leader or priest in the Anglican Church
Vishnu   Hindu god who comes to earth in different forms to save humankind from the powers of evil

W

Waheguru   'Wonderful Lord', Sikh title of God

Y

Yahrzeit   anniversary of the death of a relative, a day of remembrance and mourning
Yoga   ancient system of exercises for controlling and disciplining the body and the senses
Yom Kippur   Jewish Day of Atonement

Z

Zakah   charity alms for the poor, one of the Five Pillars of Islam

Bibliography and resources

THE
ASHCOMBE
SCHOOL
DORKING

General

Brown, A., Rankin, J. and Wood, A., *Religions*, Longman Educational

Cole, O., *Six Religions in the Twentieth Century*, Hulton Educational

Collinson, C. and Miller, C., *Milestones: Rites of Passage in a Multifaith Community*, Edward Arnold

Kennedy, B., Hasted, S. and Gormer, N., *Rites of Passage* (film strips and tapes) Stanley Thornes

World Religions: Aspects of . . . Video Text Educational and Exmouth School

Hinduism

Bahree, P., *Religions of the World: The Hindu World,* Macmillan Educational

Kanitkar, V.P. (Hemant), *Hindu Festivals and Sacraments*, Hemant

Kanitkar, V.P. (Hemant), *Religions of the World: Hinduism,* Wayland Books

Hinduism through the Eyes of Hindu Children, CEM Videos

Judaism

Charing, D., *Religions of the World: The Jewish World,* Macdonald Educational

Forta, A., *Examining Religions: Judaism,* Heinemann Educational

Wood, A., *Dictionaries of World Religions: Judaism*, Batsford Books

Judaism through the Eyes of Jewish Children, CEM Videos

Buddhism

Morgan, P., *Buddhism in the Twentieth Century*, Hulton Educational

Samarasekara, D., *I am a Buddhist*, Franklin Watts

Snelling, J., *Religions of the World: Buddhism,* Wayland Books

Christianity

Brown, A., *Religions of the World: The Christian World*, Macdonald Educational

O'Donnel, K., *Christianity: An Approach for GCSE*, Edward Arnold

People at Worship Slides Series, The Slide Centre

Islam

Sarwar, G., *Islam Beliefs and Teachings*, The Muslim Educational Trust

Tames, R., *World Religions in Education: Approaches to Islam*, John Murray

Thorley, S., *Islam in Words and Pictures*, RMEP

Islam through the Eyes of Muslim Children, CEM Videos

Sikhism

Arora, R., *Religions of the World: Sikhism*, Wayland Books

Sacha, G.S., *The Sikhs and their Way of Life*, The Sikh Missionary Society

Sikhism through the Eyes of Sikh Children, CEM Videos